SHABBAT SHALOM!

Project Directors: Claudia Kitsberg, Rabbi Michael Laitner

Project Manager: Fiona Palmer

Project Developer: Dr Daniel Rose

Editors: Annabel Ries, Rabbi Daniel Sturgess

Design: Richard Herman

With sincere thanks to: Rabbi Dr Harvey Belovski, David Collins,
Caleb Ford, Simon Goulden, Gila Howard, Joanna Rose

Print: Kellmatt Ltd

First published in Great Britain 2019 by the United Synagogue
305 Ballards Lane, Finchley, London N12 8GB
Registered charity number 242552
info@theus.org.uk
www.theus.org.uk
©2019 United Synagogue

ISBN 978-1-909004-12-2

DEDICATION

Karen & Andrew Harris and Michelle & Martin Mitchell
dedicate this wonderful book
to the merit of their dear parents z"l

MARLENE GREEN
RUTH HARRIS
DAVID HARRIS

who truly valued their Jewish roots
and inspired their families to hold close what is important in life.

A note from the Harris family...

Our family, just like many others, is on a constant journey of discovery.

With four kids and two full time careers, every few months seems to bring us fresh challenges and opportunities. About 15 years ago, we decided to make a change in our lives in order to find a way to spend more time together. So, we nominated Saturday as our 'Family Day'. This meant no football or shopping trips – instead, we would find new family activities. At first, we attended the children service at our local synagogue and invited friends over for the afternoon. We quickly started to look forward to this quality family time. Over the years, and with help from our eldest daughter, we watered these initial seeds into what has become a beautiful Shabbat experience.

Today, we cling on to Shabbat as a precious oasis, freeing us from our technology-led lives. Allowing us to see clearly again and to be 'back in the moment' with each other whilst, at the same time, recharging and re-energising us for the rest of the week.

SHABBAT SHALOM!

CONTENTS

Dedication: The Harris & Mitchell families

Introduction: Chief Rabbi Ephraim Mirvis

Welcome: Michael Goldstein

בראשית	2	**Bereishit**
בראשית	4	Bereishit
נח	6	Noach
לך לך	8	Lech Lecha
וירא	10	Vayera
חיי שרה	12	Chayei Sarah
תולדות	14	Toledot
ויצא	16	Vayeitzei
וישלח	18	Vayishlach
וישב	20	Vayeishev
מקץ	22	Mikeitz
ויגש	24	Vayigash
ויחי	26	Vayechi

שמות	28	**Shemot**
שמות	30	Shemot

וארא	32	Vaera
בא	34	Bo
בשלח	36	Beshalach
יתרו	38	Yitro
משפטים	40	Mishpatim
תרומה	42	Terumah
תצוה	44	Tetzaveh
כי תשא	46	Ki Tissa
ויקהל	48	Vayakhel
פקודי	50	Pekudei

ויקרא	52	**Vayikra**
ויקרא	54	Vayikra
צו	56	Tzav
שמיני	58	Shemini
תזריע	60	Tazria
מצורע	62	Metzora
אחרי מות	64	Acharei Mot
קדושים	66	Kedoshim

SHABBAT SHALOM!

אמור	68	Emor
בהר	70	Behar
בחקותי	72	Bechukotai

במדבר	74	**Bemidbar**
במדבר	76	Bemidbar
נשא	78	Nasso
בהעלותך	80	Beha'alotecha
שלח	82	Shelach Lecha
קרח	84	Korach
חקת	86	Chukat
בלק	88	Balak
פינחס	90	Pinchas
מטות	92	Matot
מסעי	94	Masei

דברים	96	**Devarim**
דברים	98	Devarim
ואתחנן	100	Vaetchanan
עקב	102	Eikev
ראה	104	Re'eh
שופטים	106	Shofetim
כי תצא	108	Ki Teitzei
כי תבוא	110	Ki Tavo
נצבים	112	Nitzavim
וילך	114	Vayeilech
האזינו	116	Ha'azinu
וזאת הברכה	118	Vezot Haberacha

Sedra calendar	120
Picture credits	122

INTRODUCTION

Imagine you are granted a private audience with the Monarch. It stands to reason that you would prepare for the encounter extremely carefully. You would cautiously select your clothing, ensuring that you look as presentable as possible and gather your thoughts so that the precious moments you have in the presence of royalty are used judiciously.

Once the audience has concluded and you have left the palace, you can relax. After all, there is nothing more to prepare for. The encounter has ended, the task completed.

But that was not the approach taken by Aharon, the High Priest, when he entered the Holy of Holies on *Yom Kippur* for an audience with God Himself. In fact, the High Priest changed his garments and immersed in a *mikva* on five separate occasions, including one which was after his encounter with the Divine.

Now, we can understand why Aharon purified himself as he approached the Almighty. But, why did he purify himself as he prepared to return to his regular environment?

In *Parashat Acharei Mot* we are told, *"Bezot – with this, Aharon the High Priest will enter the Holy of Holies"* (*Vayikra* 16:3). What did Aharon bring with him on this most auspicious occasion? The *Midrash* explains that Aharon entered with the merit of all the *Shabbatot* that the Jewish people had kept during the previous year, a powerful indication of the significance of our *Shabbat* observance.

As such, we can deduce that his exit must also have been *Shabbat*-related. The positive impact of *Shabbat* goes well beyond the 25 hours of its observance. *Shabbat* revitalises us physically, mentally and spiritually, empowering us to tackle the coming week with renewed vigour and enthusiasm. That is why in our *Havdala* ceremony (to mark the end of *Shabbat*), we smell the *besamim* – the spices, the fragrance of which lingers, as a symbol of the spirituality of *Shabbat* which does not dissipate, but stays with us long into the week.

This was what Aharon was preparing for. In the Holy of Holies, on the *Shabbat* of all *Shabbatot*, he had equipped himself with the spiritual tools he needed to go out into the world and change it for the better.

Every single *Shabbat* presents a wonderful opportunity for us to recharge our spiritual batteries, to spend time with those who matter most to us, to learn something and to enrich our lives.

It is in this context that *Shabbat Shalom*!, produced by the United Synagogue, will provide a wonderful contribution to our *Shabbat* experience and, of course, to ShabbatUK. Filled with fascinating thoughts and priceless insights, I have no doubt that this book will be treasured by family members of all ages. Most significantly, may the inspiration we receive every *Shabbat* from *Shabbat Shalom*! help to beautify and enhance the days that follow.

Chief Rabbi Ephraim Mirvis

WELCOME TO
SHABBAT SHALOM!

This unique *Shabbat* compendium has something for everyone, young or old, to enjoy every week of the year. *Shabbat Shalom*! is not just a fascinating book for an individual to dip in and out of, it's also designed for you to share and discuss around the *Shabbat* table.

In recent years, the enormous success of ShabbatUK has demonstrated the salience of the weekly cycle for Jews. In a world where faces are increasingly replaced by screens, and conversations are replaced with electronic messages, connecting with our family, our friends and ourselves has never been so important. Engaging with *Shabbat* enriches us. Whether or not you are a regular participant in your local shul's community life, this book provides another wonderful way to revel in our heritage.

In addition to what's contained in these pages, more content can be found on the US website at www.theus.org.uk/shabbatshalom. However you choose to use *Shabbat Shalom*! I hope you use it regularly and enjoy it to the full.

Wishing you many years of weekly discussing, sharing, learning, reading and above all enjoying this fabulous book, which I hope will enhance the *Shabbat* experience for all.

Shabbat Shalom!

Michael Goldstein
President, United Synagogue

BEREISHIT

Bereishit is kindly
sponsored by
Peter and Jacqui Zinkin

בְּרֵאשִׁית

Bereishit

1st SEDRA IN:

בְּרֵאשִׁית
Bereishit

BY NUMBERS:

146 verses
1,931 words
7,235 letters

HEADLINES:

Creation of the world

Parasha Summary

In the *Torah*'s opening *parasha*, God creates the world in six days and ceases creative work on the seventh. God sanctifies and blesses the seventh day, *Shabbat*, as a day of rest. Adam and Eve eat the forbidden fruit from the Tree of Knowledge of Good and Evil and are expelled from the Garden of Eden. Cain kills Abel and is punished accordingly. We read about the ten generations between Adam and Noah and then the degeneration of humanity, so much so that God considers destroying all of Creation.

THE STORY OF JEWISH HISTORY

If the statistics are right, the Jews constitute but one percent of the human race. It suggests a nebulous dim puff of star dust lost in the blaze of the Milky Way. Properly the Jew ought hardly to be heard of; but he is heard of, has always been heard of. He is as prominent on the planet as any other people, and his commercial importance is extravagantly out of proportion to the smallness of his bulk. His contributions to the world's list of great names in literature, science, art, music, finance, medicine and abstruse learning are also way out of proportion to the weakness of his numbers. He has made a marvellous fight in the world, in all the ages; and has done it with his hands tied behind him. He could be vain of himself and be excused for it. The Egyptian, the Babylonian and the Persian arose, filled the planet with sound and splendour, then faded to dream stuff and passed away; the Greek and Roman followed and made a vast noise, and they are gone; other peoples have sprung up and held their torch high for a while, but it burned out, and they sit in twilight now or have vanished. The Jew saw them all, beat them all, and is now what he always was, exhibiting no decadence, no infirmities of age, no weakening of his parts, no slowing of his energies, no dulling of his alert and aggressive mind.

All things are mortal but the Jew; all other forces pass, but he remains.

What is the secret of his immortality?

Mark Twain's *Essay on the Jews*, 1899

DISCUSSION QUESTIONS

1. What is the secret of Jewish continuity?

2. Is Jewish history miraculous?

For extra on these articles & more visit www.theus.org.uk/shabbatshalom

QUOTE OF THE WEEK

[My] faith [in God] has been persistently reinforced by Jewish history... 'These are His awesome effects, for were it not for awe of God, how could one nation (the Jews) survive among the nations?' (*Talmud Yoma* 69b)... our singular history has provided much reinforcement.

Rabbi Dr Aharon Lichtenstein (1933–2015)

SHABBAT
'SWITCH OFF YOUR SMARTPHONE AND SOAK UP THE SABBATH'

Sometimes the more digitally connected we are, the more disconnected we become from everything that is . important. In this context, *Shabbat* is more relevant now than ever before. It is a time to deal with real friends, people and challenges. Real relationships, whether a long overdue catch up with old friends or a joyful family meal, are strengthened by the discipline to rise above the weekly grind and experience something altogether more meaningful.

Jack Lew, an observant Jew who was Chief of Staff to US President Barack Obama, speaks often of how understanding the President was about his leaving the White House for *Shabbat*. Lew says that the President would frequently point to his watch on a Friday afternoon and prompt him that it was time to get going – "to remind me that it was important to him, not just to me, that I be able to make that balance."

Striking that balance is a worthy aspiration, not just for Jews, but for all of our society.

Chief Rabbi Mirvis

PARASHA QUIZ

1. Day 1: What did God create?
2. Day 2: What did God also call the *rakia*?
3. Day 3: What did God see twice?
4. Day 4: What are the *meorot* (luminaries/lights)?
5. Day 5: Where did the creatures created on this day live?
6. Day 6: What is the difference between the humans and all the other creations made on this day?
7. Day 7: What did God create?

Answers:
1. Light and darkness
2. The Heavens (*Shamayim*)
3. "That it was good"
4. The sun and the moon
5. In the sea and the sky
6. Humans are created "in the image of God".
7. *Shabbat* (rest)

Parasha Summary

God sends a flood to destroy the world. Only Noah, "a righteous man in his generation", his family and at least two of each living creature survive the flood by taking refuge in an ark that God commanded Noah to build. God promises never to make such a flood again. The rainbow recalls this promise. The people that then populate the world build the Tower of Babel, but it angers God and leads to the dispersal of Noah's descendants. Abram and Sarai are born, and further genealogy is listed.

2nd SEDRA IN:

בְּרֵאשִׁית

Bereishit

BY NUMBERS:

153 verses
1,861 words
6,907 letters

HEADLINES:

The flood and Tower of Babel

THE FLOOD STORY IN MIDRASH (RABBINIC TEACHINGS)

When Noach (Noah) was told by God of the impending flood and the end of the world, he begged his neighbours to repent, saying that a terrible flood was due to destroy humanity and animals because of their wickedness. Noach purposely worked slowly, hoping that the people would heed his warnings and repent. According to one teaching, Noach planted cedar trees and chopped them down over 120 years, to give the people time to change their ways. But they still did not believe him. Instead, they mocked and persecuted him.

Then Noach brought the animals into the ark, seven of each 'clean' animal but only two of the 'unclean' ones.

According to some rabbinic commentaries, Noach's faith was shaky and he did not board the ark until he stood ankle deep in water. Others assert that Noach awaited God's directions to enter, just as he awaited God's permission to leave.

Once inside, Noach was constantly occupied attending to all the animals, which fed at different times. One of the lions, angry from hunger, attacked and injured him, so he remained lame for the rest of his life.

When Noach eventually left the ark, he saw the destruction and began to weep, saying: "Lord of the world, You are merciful; why didn't You pity Your children?" God answered: "Foolish shepherd! Now you pray for the world? If you had done so when I announced to you my plans for the Flood, it would have been avoided. You knew you would be rescued, and therefore did not care for others. Now you pray?!" Noach acknowledged his fault, and brought offerings for forgiveness.

For extra on these articles & more visit www.theus.org.uk/shabbatshalom

JEWISH HISTORY
THE BALFOUR DECLARATION

The Balfour Declaration was a statement of support made by the British Government for the establishment of a national home for the Jewish people in *Eretz Yisrael*. It was written on 2 November 1917 by Lord Arthur James Balfour, former Prime Minister (1902–1905) and then Foreign Minister (1916–1919). He sent it to Lord Lionel Rothschild, a senior member of the Jewish community in Britain.

It stated: "His Majesty's Government view with favour the establishment in Palestine of a national home for the Jewish people, and will use their best endeavours to facilitate the achievement of this object, it being clearly understood that nothing shall be done which may prejudice the civil and religious rights of existing non-Jewish communities in Palestine, or the rights and political status enjoyed by Jews in any other country".

This was the first time in modern history that a great power had recognised Jewish national aspirations in *Eretz Yisrael*, and lent its support to them. It was a partial realisation of the dream of Theodore Herzl, the founder of modern Zionism, some 13 years after his death.

At the 'Balfour 100' centenary celebrations in 2017, Prime Minister Theresa May proudly restated the UK's commitment to the aims of the Declaration and to furthering the UK's relationship with Israel.

DISCUSSION QUESTION

Why was it so important to the Zionist establishment in 1917 to get official support from a great power for the Zionist cause?

BRITISH MANDATE QUIZ

1. What year did Britain conquer Palestine and from whom?
2. Who was the British General that conquered Palestine, paving the way for the establishing of the British Mandate?
3. What year did the British Mandate of Palestine begin?
4. Who was the first High Commissioner for Palestine?
5. What were the official languages of Mandatory Palestine?
6. What was the capital of Mandatory Palestine?

Answers:
1. 1917 from the Turkish Ottoman Empire
2. General Edmund Allenby
3. 1920
4. Sir Herbert Samuel
5. English, Arabic, Hebrew
6. Jerusalem

3rd SEDRA IN:

בְּרֵאשִׁית

Bereishit

BY NUMBERS:

126 verses
1,686 words
6,336 letters

HEADLINES:

Abraham in the Land

Parasha Summary

God tells Abram to leave his home and go "to a land that I will show you." He and his wife Sarai travel to Canaan (later to be the Land of Israel), but famine forces them to move to Egypt. Later they return to Canaan with great wealth, and Abram reluctantly parts ways with his nephew Lot. Abram defeats the armies of the four kings and rescues Lot whom they had taken captive. God makes a Covenant with Abram, bequeathing Canaan to his descendants. Abram marries Hagar, who gives birth to Ishmael. God changes Abram's name to Abraham, and Sarai's to Sarah. Abraham and all the men in his household are circumcised.

DVAR TORAH

God charges Abraham to leave everything behind and travel to a land that would become the inheritance of his offspring. Abraham and his wife, Sarah, accepted the mission to spread the idea of one God for all humanity. Did they succeed? At the end of their lives, did not Abraham and Sarah have only one true successor, their son, Isaac!?

Both the *Midrash* (Rabbinic teachings) and the *Talmud* make a curious comparison between the three patriarchs. Abraham related to God from the perspective of a mountain to climb, Isaac as an expansive field to be developed and Jacob as a home.

These metaphors suggest that both Abraham and Isaac focused on transmitting their teaching to the general public. Abraham imagined ascending metaphorical mountains to do God's bidding; this might discourage many from even trying. Isaac's field was defined by clear boundaries. But *Chazal* (the rabbinic sages) identified Jacob's outlook as a 'home', building on the teachings of his father and grandfather. Jacob understood the need to focus his efforts on where people live their own unique lives, their homes. The impact of Judaism in the home and public works in combination, as represented by each of the patriarchs.

Jacob's focus teaches us the importance of our homes and what we make them represent. Perhaps you are reading this book around the *Shabbat* table. The unique Jewish 'institution' of the *Shabbat* table is instrumental in sharing the beliefs and values that our people treasure. As you read this, consider the following question: How can we ensure that our homes are transmitting these beliefs and values?

Rabbi Dov and Rebbetzen Freda Kaplan

For extra on these articles & more visit www.theus.org.uk/shabbatshalom

PERSONALITY OF THE WEEK
YITZCHAK RABIN

On 12th Cheshvan in the Jewish calendar, the anniversary of the death of Yitzchak Rabin is commemorated across Israel with ceremonies and memorials. Rabin was assassinated on this date in 1995 by a political opponent who believed the peace process was endangering the security of the State of Israel.

Rabin was an elder statesman. Born in Jerusalem in 1922 to parents who had made *aliya* as early Zionist pioneers, he became an active Labour Zionist. He learnt agriculture and joined the Palmach fighting force as a teenager. He concentrated on his military career, ultimately becoming Chief of Staff in 1964, the position in which he served during the Six Day War in 1967.

After the army Rabin entered politics. He served twice as Prime Minister (1974–1977 and then from 1992 until his death in 1995). He has been described as a warrior in both war and peace, and signed the Oslo Peace Accords, for which he received the Nobel Peace Prize in 1994.

The anniversary of his death will forever be remembered as a tragic day in Israel's history, when a Jewish Prime Minister was assassinated by another Jew.

PARASHA QUIZ

1. Abram and Sarai each get a new name. What Hebrew letter is added to form their new names?
2. Where exactly did Abraham go with Lot and Sarah after he left Egypt?
3. In God's promise to Abraham, to what is the future people of Israel compared?

Answers:
1. ה
2. The Negev (southern) region of Israel
3. The stars of heaven

JEWISH HISTORY
THE KINDERTRANSPORT

Nine months before World War Two started, an effort was made to rescue more than 10,000 Jewish children from an almost certain death by the Nazis. Despite attempts at the 1938 International Evian Conference to find countries willing to accept Jews desperate to leave continental Europe, other countries including Britain continued to maintain strict immigration limits. However the shocking events of Kristallnacht in 1938 led to a change in public opinion. After a parliamentary debate on 21 November

1938, Britain agreed to take in Jewish refugee children, provided they would not be a burden on the state. Thus started the Kindertransport.

Children were then taken from Germany, Austria, Czechoslovakia and Poland and housed with families throughout the British Isles. The first group arrived at Harwich in December 1938, bringing 196 children from a destroyed Berlin Jewish orphanage. The transports ended with the outbreak of war in September 1939.

Most of the children ended up living in the UK. They were largely cared for by non-Jewish families, with the understanding that the children would be reunited with their families after the war. Tragically though, most of the children were orphaned during the War.

SEDRA:
וַיֵּרָא
Vayera

Parasha Summary

Angels visit Abraham and Sarah, who say that Sarah will soon have a baby despite her advanced age. Abraham argues with God about the destruction of Sodom and Gommorah. Lot and his daughters escape as the cities are destroyed, and Lot's wife is turned into a pillar of salt. Avimelech, king of the Philistines, tries to take Sarah as a wife, but God ensures she is released unharmed. Isaac is born, and Hagar and Ishmael are sent away. Abraham makes peace with Avimelech. Finally God tests Abraham, instructing him to sacrifice his beloved Isaac. This near-sacrifice of Isaac is called *Akeidat Yitzchak* (the binding of Isaac). Having seen Abraham's willingness to obey, God tells him to stop and sacrifice a ram instead.

4th SEDRA IN:
בְּרֵאשִׁית
Bereishit

BY NUMBERS:
147 verses
2,085 words
7,862 letters

HEADLINES:
Abraham's dilemmas

PERSONALITY OF THE WEEK
CHIEF RABBI LORD IMMANUEL JAKOBOVITS

Rabbi Immanuel Jakobovits was Chief Rabbi of the United Hebrew Congregations of the Commonwealth from 1966 to 1991. He was born in Konigsberg, Germany, in 1921 into a rabbinic family. He came to England as a teenage refugee, where he studied in Yeshivat Etz Chaim, receiving rabbinic ordination, and at London University. After serving congregations in London, he was appointed as Chief Rabbi of Ireland and later became the founding rabbi of the Fifth Avenue Synagogue, New York. He wrote his doctorate on Jewish medical ethics, now an established academic field of which he was largely the founder.

Rabbi Jakobovits began his Chief Rabbinate by placing Jewish education firmly at the top of the communal agenda. His tenure saw an enormous expansion of day schools and a resurgence of adult learning.

Described by a non-Jewish admirer as having the presence of Moses, he confidently and eloquently stated the Jewish view on issues facing British society. A friend and confidant of prime ministers, he was knighted in 1981 and raised to the peerage as Lord Jakobovits in 1987. He retired in 1991 and died unexpectedly in 1999.

Adapted from www.chiefrabbi.org

For extra on these articles & more visit www.theus.org.uk/shabbatshalom

RABBI MOSHE BEN MAIMON (RAMBAM)

The Spanish city of Córdoba sits on the highest navigable point along the Guadalquivir River near to Seville. Its Jewish community in the Middle Ages produced many fine scholars. Perhaps the most famous and impactful of these was Rabbi Moses ben Maimon, better known by the Hebrew acronym 'Rambam' or as 'Maimonides', whose writings are still widely studied.

Born in 1135, he became a foremost scholar of Jewish law, philosopher and doctor. His education started with his father. Before he was 13, the family had to flee Spain due to persecution by the fanatical Almohad sect, settling first in Fez, Morrocco and then to *Eretz Yisrael*. The desperate economic situation in *Eretz Yisrael* led the family to move to Fostat, near Cairo. There, the Rambam provided rabbinic leadership far and wide whilst also serving as the physician to the Sultan Saladin. In particular, his helped the Jewish community in Yemen avoid apostasy; to this day, the Rambam remains the primary rabbinic source for Yemenite Jewry. He advised many Jewish communities as well as teaching and publishing about medicine.

His most prominent works are his monumental *Mishneh Torah* (an early code of Jewish law) which is indispensable for understanding Jewish law, his commentary on the *Mishna* and his philosophical work, *Moreh Nevuchim* (*Guide to the Perplexed*). He passed away in 1204 and is buried in Tiberias, northern Israel.

A STORY FOR SHABBAT

Every Friday before dawn, the Rebbe of Nemirov would disappear. He was neither at home nor in any of the town's synagogues or houses of study. Once another scholar came to Nemirov. Puzzled by the Rebbe's disappearance, he asked his followers where the Rebbe was. "Where else but in heaven?" they replied. "The people of the town need peace, sustenance, health. The Rebbe is a holy man and he is surely in heaven, pleading our cause."

The scholar scoffed and was determined to find the Rebbe. One Thursday evening he hid in the Rebbe's house. Early the next morning he heard the Rebbe weep and sigh, then dress in peasant clothes. The Rebbe picked up an axe and went out. Stealthily, the scholar followed the Rebbe as he walked through the town and into the forest. He chopped down a tree, split it into firewood, bundled it up and walked back to town.

He stopped at a run-down cottage in a back street and knocked on the door. An ill, elderly peasant woman opened the door. 'I am Vassily,' the Rebbe said. 'I have firewood to sell, very cheap, next to nothing.' 'But I have no money,' replied the woman. 'I will give it to you on credit,' he said. 'How will I be able to pay you?' she said. 'I trust you – and do you not trust God? He will find a way of seeing that I am repaid.' 'The Rebbe helped her to light a fire, reciting the morning prayers under his breath as he did so. Then he returned home.

The scholar stayed in the town and became one of the Rebbe's disciples. Whenever he heard people say that the Rebbe ascended to heaven, he no longer laughed, but added, "And maybe even higher".

חַיֵּי שָׂרָה

Chayei Sarah

Parasha Summary

Although this *parasha*'s name means 'the life of Sarah', our Biblical matriarch dies at its start, aged 127. Abraham buys the Cave of Machpela in Hebron for her burial. It is still there today. Abraham sends his servant back to Abraham's original family to find a bride for Isaac. At a well, Rebecca impresses the servant with her kindness by offering to draw water for his camels. He meets Rebecca's family, then takes her to Isaac. They fall in love and marry. Abraham takes another wife and later dies at the age of 175. His sons Isaac and Ishmael bury him in Machpela, alongside Sarah.

5th SEDRA IN:

בְּרֵאשִׁית

Bereishit

BY NUMBERS:

105 verses
1,402 words
5,314 letters

HEADLINES:

Isaac and
Rebecca

THE BETA ISRAEL
(ETHIOPIAN JEWISH COMMUNITY IN ISRAEL)

On 29 Cheshvan every year, Jews in Israel of Ethiopian descent celebrate the festival of *Sigd*. Its name comes from *sgida* (prostration), and it is a renewal of the covenant between the Jewish people, God and the *Torah*. It was made an official national holiday in 2008. Today, since most of Ethiopian Jewry has made *aliya*, members of the community make a pilgrimage to Jerusalem during *Sigd*. It serves as an annual gathering of the entire Ethiopian community, who view it as an opportunity to strengthen the connection with their roots and culture. The *Kessim* (religious leaders), dressed in their traditional robes, carry the *Torah* scrolls under multi-coloured umbrellas, reading from the Bible and reciting prayers.

The *Beta Israel* (House of Israel) community lived in northern and northwestern Ethiopia, in more than 500 small villages, surrounded by a hostile Muslim and Christian population. The *Beta Israel* renewed contacts with other Jewish communities in the late 20th century, and the Israeli and American governments mounted *aliya* operations to transport them to Israel. These included Operations Moses and Joshua in the 1980s and Operation Solomon in the 1990s. About 120,000 *Beta Israel* live in Israel today.

For extra on these articles & more visit www.theus.org.uk/shabbatshalom

QUIZ

How did the following countries vote in the UN Partition Plan for Palestine?

1. United Kingdom
2. United States
3. Soviet Union
4. Iran
5. Argentina
6. Cuba
7. France
8. Australia
9. Venezuela
10. Poland

Answers:
1. Abstention
2. In favour
3. In favour
4. Against
5. Abstention
6. Against
7. In favour
8. In favour
9. In favour
10. In favour

Gena Turgel was born in Cracow, Poland, in 1923. She survived the horrific conditions of the Plaszow labour camp, Auschwitz and a death march with her mother in 1945 from Auschwitz to Buchenwald and then Bergen-Belsen. On 15 April 1945, the British Army liberated Bergen-Belsen. One of the British troops was Norman Turgel. On 7 October 1945, Gena and Norman were married by Rev Leslie Hardman at a synagogue in Lubeck, Germany, which the Nazis had used as a stable. After the war, Gena and Norman set up home in North West London. A member of Stanmore & Canons Park Synagogue, where her grandson Jonny is the Chazan, Gena was one of a group of dedicated Holocaust survivors who speak at schools and other venues as Holocaust educators. Her autobiography, *I Light A Candle*, was first published in 1987. She passed away in 2018.

JEWISH HISTORY
THE UN PARTITION PLAN FOR PALESTINE

Following Britain's announcement in February 1947 of its intention to terminate its Mandate government, the UN General Assembly appointed a special committee, the United Nations Special Committee on Palestine. UNSCOP recommended the establishment of two separate states, Jewish and Arab, to be joined by economic union, with the Jerusalem-Bethlehem region as an enclave under international administration.

On 29 November 1947 the UN General Assembly voted on the partition plan, adopted by 33 votes to 13 with 10 abstentions. The Jewish leadership accepted the UN plan for the establishment of two states. The Arabs rejected it and initiated military preparations to counter the declaration of a Jewish state. While strictly speaking the plan was never implemented because of this, the vote gave David Ben-Gurion and his government the legal justification for declaring independence, which he did on the last day of the British Mandate, 14 May 1948.

ILAN RAMON

Colonel Ilan Ramon, of blessed memory, was one of the Israeli Air Force pilots who bombed the nuclear reactor in Iraq in 1981, removing that threat to Israel's existence. In 2003, he joined the American crew of the space shuttle Columbia to serve as the first Israeli astronaut. Tragically, the entire crew perished when the shuttle exploded whilst returning to earth.

As the first Israeli astronaut, Ramon understood how he could represent the Jewish people to a global audience, even though he was not conventionally observant. Amongst the few possessions he took with him was a miniature *Sefer Torah*. It had miraculously been used at a clandestine *bar mitzvah* service at the Bergen Belsen concentration camp in 1944 and eventually made its way to Israel after the war along with the *bar mitzvah* boy, Joachim Joseph.

Ramon reached out to Rabbi Zvi Konikov, of Chabad of the Space & Treasure Coasts in Florida, who helped him plan how to keep *Shabbat* and *kashrut* in space. "Ilan was a very special Jew," recalls Rabbi Konikov. "He wanted to do everything in the very best way possible Jewishly... who left a strong impact on Jews all over the world."

Ilan Ramon remains an Israeli hero and an inspiration to generations of Jews.

Rabbi Konikov wrote a moving article about Ilan Ramon www.chabad.org/library/article_cdo/aid/632169/jewish/Shabbat-in-Space.htm

SEDRA:

תּוֹלְדֹת

Toledot

6th SEDRA IN:

בְּרֵאשִׁית

Bereishit

BY NUMBERS:

106 verses
1,432 words
5,426 letters

HEADLINES:

Jacob and Esau

Parasha Summary

Rebecca has twins, Esau and Jacob, who are very different characters. Esau gives Jacob his birthright in exchange for some stew. Isaac moves to the Philistines' area where he digs wells, resulting in friction between him and the locals. King Avimelech is led to think that Rebecca is Isaac's sister and later finds out she is really his wife. Later, the ageing Isaac plans to bless Esau, his firstborn. Rebecca is deeply worried as Esau is not a suitable recipient. She and Jacob organise matters so that Jacob receives the blessing instead. Esau threatens to kill Jacob, who then flees to Charan at the behest of and with the blessing of his parents.

ISRAEL
MOUNT MORIAH

Mount Moriah in Jerusalem, today known as the Temple Mount, was the site of both Temples.

Perhaps one of the best-known events in the *Torah*, the *Akeida* (Binding of Isaac), happened there. God commanded Abraham, "Take your son, your only one, who you love – Isaac – and go to the land of Moriah and offer him up on one of the mountains, which I will tell to you."

Bereishit tells us that Abraham "saw the place from afar". How did he recognise this mountain "from afar"? The Rabbis teach us that he saw a cloud on it, representing the *shechina* (Divine Presence).

Sharon Nakar

TOLEDOT QUIZ

ת   What ת is used to describe Yaakov (an איש...)?

ו   What ו is the first word of the *parasha*?

ל   What ל does Yaakov offer Eisav to eat?

ד   Yitzchak blesses Yaakov with a lot of what ד?

ו   Whose name ends with a ו because (according to Rashi) he was born in a 'complete' state (i.e. with the hair of an adult)?

ת   What ת does God tell Rivka she has in her womb?

Answers:
תם – ת (a simple man)
ואלה – ו (and these)
לחם – ל (bread)
דגן – ד (grain)
עשיו – ו – the ו which takes the root ע-שׂ-ה (make) and turns the word into 'made', as in 'fully made' (Rashi on *Bereishit* 25:25)
תומים – ת (twins)

For extra on these articles & more visit www.theus.org.uk/shabbatshalom

THE POWER OF YOUTH

In late summer of 1999 I was in Pristina making a television programme about the aftermath of the Kosovo campaign. Outside every church was a NATO tank. At the start of the conflict it had been the Serbian Christians who had attacked mosques. Now they feared reprisals from the returning refugees. The mood was tense. Murders were taking place every night. Revenge was in the air. The most important task was to establish order and a return to civil peace.

I interviewed General Sir Michael Jackson, then head of the NATO forces. To my surprise, he thanked me for what 'my people' had done. The Jewish community had taken charge of the city's 23 primary schools. It was, he said, the most valuable contribution to the city's welfare. When 800,000 people have become refugees and then return home, the most reassuring sign that life has returned to normal is that the schools open on time. That, he said, we owe to the Jewish people. Meeting the head of the Jewish community later that day, I asked him how many Jews were there currently in Pristina. His answer? Eleven.

the beauty and healing power of kindness extended across the borders of faith...

The story, as I later uncovered it, was fascinating. In the early days of the conflict, the State of Israel had, along with many international aid agencies, sent a field medical team to work with the Kosovan Albanian refugees. Immediately they noticed something others had missed. The aid agencies were concentrating, not unnaturally, on the adults. There was no one working with the children. Traumatised by the conflict and far from home, they were running wild.

The team phoned back to Israel and asked for young volunteers. Virtually every youth group in Israel, from the most secular to the most religious, sent out teams of youth leaders at two-week intervals. They worked with the children, organising summer camps, sports competitions, drama and music events and everything else they could think of to make their temporary exile feel like a summer holiday. At all levels it was an extraordinary effort. The Kosovan Albanians were Muslims, and for many of the Israeli youth workers it was their first contact and friendship with children of another faith. Their effort won high praise from UNICEF, the United Nations children's organisation. It was in the wake of this that 'the Jewish people' – Israel, the American-based 'Joint' and other Jewish agencies – were asked to supervise the return to normality of the school system in Pristina.

That episode taught me many things: the force of chesed, acts of kindness; the beauty and healing power of kindness extended across the borders of faith; and the way young people can rise to great moral achievements if we set them a challenge. The entire relief effort in Kosovo was a wonderful convergence of many people and agencies, from many faiths and nations.

Rabbi Jonathan Sacks,
To Heal a Fractured World

7th SEDRA IN:

בְּרֵאשִׁית
Bereishit

BY NUMBERS:

148 verses
2,021 words
7,512 letters

HEADLINES:

Birth of 11 of the 12 tribes

Parasha Summary

Jacob flees from his home in the Land of Israel to his uncle Laban's home, as his brother Esau has sworn to kill him. On the way he dreams that angels go up and down a ladder connecting earth to heaven. God appears to Jacob and renews the Covenants made with Abraham and Isaac. Jacob sees Rachel, Laban's daughter, tending sheep and falls in love with her. But after seven years of labour, Laban tricks Jacob into marrying his elder daughter, Leah. Committing to work for another seven years, Jacob is allowed to marry Rachel as well, but there is tension between the sisters. Leah, unloved, is blessed with children; Rachel, loved, is not. Jacob has many sons with Leah and two maidservants, but Rachel is unable to conceive. Finally, God blesses Rachel and she has a son, whom she names Joseph. Eventually, Jacob flees again, this time homeward.

QUOTE OF THE WEEK

Every Sabbath, the individual sheds the trappings of secular life. "With the Sabbath, comes rest". The soul begins to free itself of its heavy shackles. It seeks higher paths, spiritual acquisitions befitting its nature.

Rabbi Avraham Yitzchak HaCohen Kook (1865–1935)

JEWISH HISTORY
THE DEATH OF RAVINA II AND THE END OF THE TALMUDIC PERIOD

On 13 Kislev 4235 (499 CE), the co-author of the *Talmud*, Ravina II, died. This signified the end of the *Talmudic* period. Ravina II was head of Sura, the *Talmudic* academy in Babylon. Ravina I (his uncle) with Rav Ashi began the process of editing the *Gemara* that was written in Babylon. Various *Talmudic* sages continued this process, the last of which was Ravina II. This monumental work was completed in 475 CE. It involved collecting and editing the discussions, debates and rulings of hundreds of scholars and sages that had taken place in the more than 200 years since the compilation of the *Mishna* by Rabbi Judah HaNasi in approximately 180 CE. After Ravina II, no further additions were made to the *Talmud*, with the exception of the minimal editing by the Rabbanan Savura'i (476–560). This date thus marks the point at which the *Talmud* was 'closed' and became the basis for all further development of Jewish law.

For extra on these articles & more visit www.theus.org.uk/shabbatshalom

PERSONALITY OF THE WEEK
GOLDA MEIR

Golda Meir was born in 1898 in Kiev. When she was 8, her family escaped Russia during the pogroms and went to Milwaukee, USA. Golda immediately discovered an interest in activism, organising the 'American Young Sisters Society', which raised money to buy books for fellow students who couldn't afford them.

On leaving school, instead of working in her parents' deli and getting married as expected, she went to live with her sister in Denver, where she met Morris Meyerson. They married in 1917 and planned to make *Aliya*, but were delayed until 1921 when transatlantic travel resumed after World War One. They first lived on a *kibbutz*, where Golda developed her leadership skills, excelling in community responsibilities.

They later moved to Jerusalem where Golda started as a *kibbutz* representative to the *Histadrut* (Israeli labour organisation) and became a recognised spokesperson for the Zionist cause during World War Two.

In January 1948, Golda went to the USA to fundraise. Covering 17 cities in the first two weeks, her inspiring oratory raised an incredible $20 million for the Jewish Agency, three times the initial goal.

She was a signatory of Israel's Declaration of Independence in May 1948 and received the first ever Israeli passport. In 1949 the Knesset first convened, with Golda as the Labour Minister. In 1956 she became Foreign Minister and, under a directive that all foreign-service members Hebraicize their names, she changed her surname from Meyerson to Meir.

In 1966, Golda became ill and stepped down from the Cabinet, becoming General Secretary of the party. Three years later, Prime Minister Eshkol died suddenly and she was nominated to replace him. As Prime Minister she became known as the 'Iron Lady' of Israeli politics. She built a strong relationship with the US, promoted her vision for peace in the Middle East and led Israel during the 1972 terrorist attack at the Munich Olympics. Golda resigned in 1974 after the bitter Yom Kippur War of 1973 and died in 1978.

Claudia Kitsberg

QUIZ

1. Which came first, the *Mishna* or the *Gemara*?
2. The *Mishna* was the first ever attempt to write down what?
3. Who collected and edited the contents of the *Mishna*?
4. True or false: Rashi wrote a complete commentary on the entire *Talmud*?

Answers:
1. *Mishna*
2. The *Oral Torah*
3. Rabbi *Yehuda Hanasi* (Rabbi Judah the Prince)
4. False: He died before completing all volumes. Those with an incomplete Rashi commentary have a commentary from others, mostly written by his grandson, the Rashbam.

DISCUSSION QUESTIONS

1. If *Shabbat* is supposed to be a spiritual day, why do we invest so much in physical pleasure such as good food and nice clothes?

2. What can you do this week to make *Shabbat* more spiritual?

8th SEDRA IN:
בְּרֵאשִׁית
Bereishit

BY NUMBERS:

153 verses
1,976 words
7,458 letters

HEADLINES:

Jacob in the Land

Parasha Summary

Jacob prepares to meet Esau again, as he returns home after decades away. Jacob becomes afraid so he divides his camp into two, prays to God and sends gifts to Esau. On the way, he wrestles with a 'man' (perhaps an angel) who gives Jacob the additional name of Israel and blesses him. Jacob and Esau meet and part peacefully. Dinah, Jacob's daughter, is captured by Shechem, the son of the local chief, and Jacob's sons Simeon and Levi take revenge. Rachel dies giving birth to Benjamin and is buried in Beit Lechem. Isaac also dies, and is buried by his sons in the Cave of Machpela. Jacob and Esau's descendants are listed at the end of the *parasha*.

DVAR TORAH

Vayishlach introduces us to the battle between what is understood to be Esau's angel and Jacob. Jacob's struggle arose because he was alone – alone with his fears. It is comparable to the struggle we might face when we are alone, separated from our family or any social support, to live according to our moral values.

When Rabbi Yochanan Ben Zakai was close to death, the *Talmud* reports that his students asked him for a blessing. He said, "May your fear of heaven be like your fear of humans." The students were surprised. "That's all? That's the level of fear we should aspire to?" He said, "If it were only that much! When people sin, they say, 'I hope nobody is looking.'"

When we are with friends or family, we feel more responsibility for our actions. When our 'personal brand' is on the line, we do our best not to disappoint our peers.

Jacob was victorious in his struggle but did not come out of it unscathed; the angel injured Jacob's thigh. If Jacob had not been alone, he would have had the strength to overcome the angel completely.

It is best to avoid being 'alone'. We need a peer group that expects the best from us; even the greatest amongst us can be tempted. Pursue friendships and check in regularly with your friends, especially when you feel you or they are alone. The strength we gain from our peers helps us to increase our spirituality and continue to grow!

Rabbi Aharon Zerbib

DISCUSSION QUESTIONS

1. Jacob believed Esau was marching to fight and kill him. Do you think that siblings would really want to fight and even kill each other? Can you explain why?

2. What do you think that the story of Jacob struggling with the angel means?

3. Why do you think Jacob's additional name, Yisrael, became the name for which all his descendants become known (*Bnei Yisrael*)?

For extra on these articles & more visit www.theus.org.uk/shabbatshalom

PERSONALITY OF THE WEEK
CHIEF RABBI DR JOSEPH H HERTZ

Rabbi Hertz was born in Hungary in 1872 and moved to America as child. He was a rabbi in Johannesburg, from where he had been deported by the Boers for being pro-British, then moved to Orach Chayim Congregation in New York. He was installed as Chief Rabbi of the United Hebrew Congregations of the Empire in 1913.

World War One broke out soon after and its problems and opportunities dominated the early years of his tenure. His thundering and courageous support for the Zionist movement led to a decisive intervention in May 1917 during the negotiations leading to the Balfour Declaration, while concern for the pastoral wellbeing of Jewish troops caused Rabbi Hertz to write *A Book of Jewish Thoughts*, the first of his major literary works.

In 1920, Rabbi Hertz undertook the first pastoral tour of Empire Jewry, to 42 communities across South Africa, Australia, New Zealand and Canada. The prestige that accrued both to Rabbi Hertz and his office was immeasurable. He was later made a Companion of Honour.

Rabbi Hertz's most lasting monuments are his English commentaries on the *Torah* and prayer book, conveying traditional Jewish interpretations in a way that is accessible to all. Still in use, they remain his major contribution to Jewish scholarship and his best known works. He died in office in 1946.

Adapted from www.chiefrabbi.org

QUIZ: JEWISH SCIENTISTS

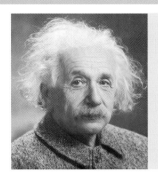

1. Which famous medieval philosopher and *Talmud*ist was also a famous physician?
2. Who was the father of modern psychoanalysis?
3. Who was the Danish physicist who made fundamental contributions to understanding atomic structure and quantum mechanics?
4. Who is arguably the most famous scientist in history?
5. Which chemist invented a way to make acetone, vital in the British effort in World War One, and later became the first President of the State of Israel?

Answers:
1. Rambam/Maimonides
2. Sigmund Freud
3. Niels Bohr
4. Albert Einstein
5. Chaim Weizmann

ISRAEL
THE FIRST KIBBUTZ

On 18 Kislev 5670 (1909) the first *kibbutz* was established on the shores of the Kinneret. Kibbutz Degania was founded by ten men and two women at a place known as Umm Juni. In June 1912, the group moved from the mud huts and wooden shack of Umm Juni to a new stone-built compound, at its permanent location where the Jordan River emerges from the Sea of Galilee. Prominent early Zionist leaders and personalities worked and lived in Degania, such as the poetess Rachel Bluwstein, the Zionist thinker AD Gordon and the soldier Joseph Trumpledor. The soldier and political leader Moshe Dayan was the second baby born on Degania. In 1920 a second *kibbutz* was founded nearby and called Degania Bet, while the original *kibbutz* became known as Degania Alef. Today it is home to about 750 people.

SEDRA:
וַיֵּשֶׁב
Vayeishev

Parasha Summary

Jacob favours his son Joseph and gives him a special coat. Joseph also has dreams of grandeur, so his brothers resent him. When the brothers go to tend their flocks, Jacob sends Joseph to join them. The brothers discuss murdering Joseph, but instead Joseph is sold into slavery. The brothers lead Jacob to believe that Joseph had been killed, and he is distraught.

Tamar successively marries two of Judah's sons, each of whom dies. Judah does not allow her levirate marriage to his youngest son.

Joseph ends up in Egypt as a slave yet remains righteous. His master Potiphar's wife gets him imprisoned, where he interprets dreams.

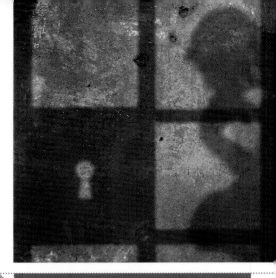

9th SEDRA IN:
בְּרֵאשִׁית
Bereishit

BY NUMBERS:
112 verses
1,558 words
5,972 letters

HEADLINES:
Joseph's dreams and being sold into slavery

QUOTE OF THE WEEK

A person is only shown in his dreams the thoughts of his heart.

One view in the Babylonian Talmud, Berachot 55b

DISCUSSION QUESTION

Do you think dreams are a reflection of what is in your subconscious or do dreams have meaning beyond that?

RASHI ON CHANUKAH

The great scholar Rashi (Rabbi Shlomo ben Yitzchaki, 1040–1105) writes that the main miracle of *Chanukah* was the miracle of the oil. Yet the military victory over the Greeks seems to be a much greater miracle and maintained our religious autonomy.

Rabbi Chaim Shmulevitz (1902–1979) explains Rashi's position. The miracle of oil was technically unnecessary since we could have waited for fresh supplies of oil to arrive at the Temple. Instead, that miracle demonstrated that God was not content simply to give us the 'basics', such as life itself and religious independence, but in fact God wanted us to have things that are not absolutely necessary. Therefore, we light the number of candles corresponding to each night of *Chanukah*, which is beyond the basic requirement of one candle per night, to show our commitment is greater than the basic requirement.

Rabbi Daniel Fine

For extra on these articles & more visit www.theus.org.uk/shabbatshalom

JEWISH HISTORY
CHANUKAH

The eight-day festival of *Chanukah* commemorates the rededication during the 2nd century BCE of the Second Temple in Jerusalem, when the Jews rose up against the Greek-Syrians in the Maccabean revolt. The word *Chanukah* means 'dedication', as the Temple was rededicated on 25 Kislev.

Around 200 BCE, Judea came under the control of Antiochus III, the Seleucid king of Syria, who allowed the Jews to continue practising their religion. But his son, Antiochus IV Epiphanes, outlawed the Jewish religion and ordered the Jews to worship Greek gods. In 168 BCE, his soldiers attacked Jerusalem, massacring thousands of people and desecrating the Temple.

Matityahu the *Cohen* and his five sons led a rebellion against Antiochus. When Matityahu died in 166 BCE his son Yehuda, known as Yehuda the Maccabee (Hammer), took over. Within two years the Jews had driven the Greek-Syrians out of Jerusalem. They purified the Second Temple, rebuilt its altar and lit its *menorah*.

Even though there was only enough ritually pure olive oil to keep the *menorah* burning for a single day, the flames continued burning for eight nights, allowing enough time to find a fresh supply. This miraculous event inspired the Jewish sages to proclaim a yearly eight-day festival called *Chanukah*.

Eliezer Ben-Yehuda was the father of the revival of Hebrew as a modern language. This coincided with the birth of modern Zionism, for which Hebrew as a spoken language and Hebrew culture was fundamentally important.

Ben-Yehuda was born Eliezer Yitzchak Perlman in Belorussia to a religious family. He became obsessed with reviving the Hebrew language as a tool to unite all Jews in *Eretz Yisrael*.

He studied at the Sorbonne in Paris and made *aliya* in 1881 with other early pioneers. He began teaching Hebrew, working day and night to develop a new language that could replace Yiddish or Ladino as the language of everyday communication between Jews in *Eretz Yisrael*. The most important task was to create new words for the language of the Bible to be usable for day-to-day modern life. He did this by using the rules of grammar and linguistic analogy from Semitic roots such as Biblical Hebrew, Aramaic and Arabic. His greatest accomplishment was the creation of a modern Hebrew dictionary.

Leading by example, he spoke to his son, Ben-Zion, only in Hebrew.

QUIZ: BEN-YEHUDA'S NEW HEBREW WORDS

1. 'Doll' inspired by the Arabic word bu'bu (little child/doll)
2. 'Dictionary', inspired by a new conjugate of מִלָּה (word)
3. 'Road', based on the *Mishnaic* word kvisha (side path)
4. 'Butterfly', inspired by the Hebrew verb לְפַרְפֵּר (to flutter)
5. 'Bicycle', inspired by the Biblical word אוֹפַן (wheel)
6. 'Pink', inspired by the Hebrew word, itself from the ancient Persian, וֶרֶד (rose)
7. 'Train', inspired by the Biblical רֶכֶב (caravan of vehicles)

Answers
1. בֻּבָּה (buba)
2. מִלּוֹן (milon)
3. כְּבִיש (kvish)
4. פַּרְפַּר (parpar)
5. אוֹפַנַּיִם (ofanayim)
6. וֶרוֹד (varod)
7. רַכֶּבֶת (rakevet)

מִקֵּץ
Mikeitz

10th SEDRA IN:
בְּרֵאשִׁית
Bereishit

BY NUMBERS:
146 verses
2,022 words
7,914 letters

HEADLINES:
Joseph rises to prominence

Parasha Summary

Pharaoh has two troubling dreams. At the suggestion of his baker, who remembers Joseph from prison, Pharaoh brings Joseph to interpret them. Having told Pharaoh that the dreams warn of eventual drought and famine, he then announces a solution to the problem. Pharaoh is so impressed he appoints Joseph to high office in Egypt, second only to himself. There is then a famine, and Jacob sends his sons, minus Benjamin, to Egypt to buy food. The brothers do not recognise Joseph when they meet him, and Joseph tests them by accusing them of being spies. Joseph arrests Simeon and demands the brothers bring Benjamin to Egypt to prove they are not spies. When Benjamin arrives, Joseph puts a goblet in Benjamin's bag and accuses him of stealing it.

ℚUOTE OF THE WEEK

If you only have enough money to buy either *Shabbat* candles or wine for *kiddush* or *Chanukah* candles, then you should buy *Shabbat* candles, because they create *shalom bayit* (domestic peace).

Babylonian Talmud, Shabbat 23b

DISCUSSION QUESTIONS

1. How do you think *Shabbat* candles can provide *shalom* in your house?

2. How is the message of *Shabbat* different from the message of *Chanukah*? Which do you think should take precedence?

3. *Shabbat* is a time when blessings are given to children. Why do you think this is so?

For extra on these articles & more visit www.theus.org.uk/shabbatshalom

CHANUKAH AND AL HANISIM

"What is the first thing you would buy if I'd given you a winning lottery ticket?" I once asked a primary school student. The pupil looked up at me sweetly and responded, "Rabbi Feldman, I would buy you a thank you card, of course, for giving me the ticket!"

The specific placement of the *Al Hanisim* ('Concerning the miracles') paragraph, which we add into the *Amida* and *Birkat Hamazon* prayers during *Chanukah*, is instructive. This extra text, highlighting the open miracle of *Chanukah*, is inserted next to the existing blessings of gratitude. It helps us to express gratitude for – and celebrate the miracles of – *Chanukah*.

The point to consider, though, is one of causality. Which is the trigger for greater appreciation? Does the placing of *Al Hanisim* near the regularly recited blessings of gratitude encourage a greater appreciation for the miracle of *Chanukah* as it is mentioned within a context of general appreciation? Or does the placing of *Al Hanisim* near these two more general blessings encourage a greater sense of gratitude for the everyday gifts from God?

Perhaps the answer is that both the ordinary and the extraordinary are needed to develop our sense of gratitude. It is specifically the combination of seeing God's hand in both the everyday and in the miraculous that engenders a deep sense of thankfulness. *Chanukah* is the time of year when all the goodness we receive is more illuminated – and that is certainly a reason to say thank you.

Rabbi Elchonon Feldman

PERSONALITY OF THE WEEK
CHIEF RABBI DR HERMANN ADLER (1839–1911)

Rabbi Adler was educated in London, Leipzig and Vienna. The recipient of rabbinic ordination as well as a PhD, he stood in for his father, Nathan Marcus HaCohen Adler, as Chief Rabbi when the latter's health declined in 1879, before succeeding his father in 1891.

He developed the ethos of both the United Synagogue and much of the British Jewish community. In particular, he led the community in assisting the large numbers of poverty-stricken Jewish immigrants from Eastern Europe to build new lives in the UK. He also raised funds to help Jews in need elsewhere, including the Land of Israel, as well as for the relief of general poverty in the UK.

He was President of Jews' College, Rabbi of the Great Synagogue in Duke's Place and the acknowledged representative of British Jewry in non-Jewish circles.

CHANUKAH QUIZ

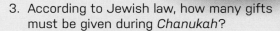

1. What does the word *Chanukah* mean?

2. Who is the Greek-Syrian leader who tried to destroy Judaism?

3. According to Jewish law, how many gifts must be given during *Chanukah*?

4. Why do we eat doughnuts and latkes on *Chanukah*?

5. How many candles (excluding the *shamash*) are lit in total during *Chanukah*?

6. Who is the best-known hero of the *Chanukah* story and what does his name mean?

7. How many branches does a *chanukia* have?

8. How many branches did the *menorah* in the Temple have?

9. What four letters are on the *dreidel*?

10. What do they stand for and what does that mean?

Answers:
1. Dedication
2. Antiochus Epiphanes
3. 0
4. Because they are fried in oil which reminds us of the miracle of the oil
5. 36
6. Yehuda Hamaccabee – Judah the Hammer
7. 8 (usually plus the *shamash*)
8. 7
9. נ,ג,ה,פ(or ש instead of פ in Israel)
10. נס גדול היה שם/פה – A great miracle happened there/here

11th SEDRA IN:

בְּרֵאשִׁית

Bereishit

BY NUMBERS:

106 verses
1,480 words
5,680 letters

HEADLINES:

Jacob and his family coming to Egypt

Parasha Summary

Last week's *parasha* ended with the dramatic cliff-hanger: Joseph's brothers pleading to save their youngest brother, Benjamin, from prison. But why did Joseph give them such a hard time?

Now in *Vayigash*, Judah opens his heart to Joseph, who was masked as the viceroy of Egypt. Judah retells the family story in great detail, almost as if Joseph had not been there. With great courage, Judah offered himself as a prisoner instead of Benjamin, to spare their father further anguish.

Only then did Joseph reveal his identity and reunite the family.

Joseph saw that his brothers had truly changed and had done suitable *teshuva* (repentance) for selling him. It is as if he knew the insightful words of the Rambam, who later wrote that true repentance comes when a person is put in the same situation as when he sinned in the past, but this time acts with righteousness instead of sin. Joseph had perhaps orchestrated this chain of events so that brothers could be faced with a similar situation – the choice of abandoning a brother, just like they had done with him.

This repentance produced peace and unity amongst the brothers, so they could form the beginnings of our nation, the Children of Israel.

Rabbi Marc Levene

PERSONALITY OF THE WEEK
ROSALIND FRANKLIN

Rosalind Franklin (1920–1958) is well-known and remembered for her scientific discoveries and significant contribution to the understanding of the structure of DNA. She was born in London to an influential Jewish family; her great uncle, Herbert Samuel, was in fact the first practising Jewish member of the British Cabinet.

Her interest in science sparked during her time at St Paul's Girls' School where she excelled at maths and science and decided at the age of 15 that she wanted to be a scientist. She went on to study at Newnham College, Cambridge where she received a fellowship for research into physical chemistry. During World War Two she gave up her own research to dedicate herself to contribution to the war effort, for example through her investigations into the uses of carbon and coal in battle.

Later on, in 1951, she turned her attention to DNA structure and X-ray diffraction, conducting research at King's College. Prior to her embarking on this project, very little was known about the topic. Her discoveries were momentous, completely changing the understanding of DNA. She found the density of DNA and its helical formation. During this period the famous 'Photograph 51' was taken which laid the foundations for the ground-breaking discovery that the structure of DNA is a double-helix polymer.

In 1956 Franklin was diagnosed with ovarian cancer yet she did not let this interrupt her experiments. Determined to continue with her breakthroughs in physical chemistry, Franklin continued working up until just a few weeks before her death on 16 April 1958, aged just 37.

Nicole Kitsberg

For extra on these articles & more visit www.theus.org.uk/shabbatshalom

QUOTE OF THE WEEK

What is meant by honouring *Shabbat*? The sages explained this by declaring that each person should wash his face, hands and feet with hot water on Friday in honour of the *Shabbat*, then enwrap himself in a garment and be seated with dignity in expectation of the Sabbath, receiving it as if he were coming out to meet the king. The ancient sages used to assemble their disciples on Friday, put on their best clothes and say: "Come, let us go out to meet King *Shabbat*."

**Rambam, *Mishneh Torah*,
The Laws of Shabbat, 30:2**

JEWISH HISTORY
THE TENTH OF TEVET

On 10 Tevet 588 BCE, the siege of Jerusalem by Nebuchadnezzar II of Babylonia began — an event that culminated in the destruction of the first Temple. Approximately two and a half years later, on 17 Tammuz, the walls of Jerusalem were breached. Three weeks after that, on 9 Av, the Temple was destroyed. The rabbis instituted all three of these days as fast days, for prayer and introspection.

DISCUSSION QUESTIONS

1. Why do you think the rabbis instituted fast days on days of national mourning and tragedy?

2. What is the purpose of a fast?

QUIZ: THE LAND OF ISRAEL DIVIDED INTO THE 12 TRIBES

1. Which tribes were located on the east bank of the River Jordan?

2. Which tribe has the smallest allocation of land?

3. In which tribe's territory is today's Tel Aviv?

4. Which tribe did not have an ancestral territory?

5. Which tribes formed the southern kingdom of Judah?

6. Which two tribes came from one of Jacob's sons?

Answers:
1. Reuben, Gad and part of Menashe
2. Zebulun
3. Dan
4. Levi
5. Judah and Benjamin
6. Ephraim and Menashe

12th SEDRA IN:

בְּרֵאשִׁית

Bereishit

BY NUMBERS:

85 verses
1,158 words
4,448 letters

HEADLINES:

The final years of Jacob and Joseph

Parasha Summary

Vayechi brings the book of Genesis, which contains much family conflict and tension, to a serene conclusion. Joseph reassures Jacob that he will be buried in the Land of Israel. Jacob on his death bed blesses Joseph's sons and then his own 12 sons. Jacob is buried in the Cave of Machpela in Hebron, alongside his parents, grandparents and wife, Leah. We are taught that Adam and Eve are buried there too. The Cave of Machpela remains a sacred religious site and place of prayer for Jews. It is also venerated by Muslims.

Joseph forgives his brothers a second time. Prior to his death he assures them that God will eventually bring the family back to Israel and requests that his remains are taken back to Israel when the Exodus will take place. As *Bereishit* ends and *Shemot* begins, the *Torah* transitions to a new period: the birth of Israel as a nation.

ISRAEL
MOUNT HERZL

In this week's *parasha* we hear for the last time in the *Torah* about the famous burial plot of the patriarchs – the Cave of Machpela in Hebron, which is still a deeply important site for Jews today. For many years, until after the Six Day War of 1967, Jews were refused entry to the Cave.

There are also other, modern cemeteries which have importance to the Jewish people. Mount Herzl in Jerusalem is one such place.

Mount Herzl is Israel's national cemetery, where the nation's presidents, prime ministers, speakers of the Knesset and other dignitaries are buried. It is also the largest military cemetery in Israel. In 1949, when soldiers who fell in the Jerusalem area were buried on Mount Herzl, the Government decided to turn the mount into the main cemetery for IDF soldiers who fall in the line of duty.

At the bottom of Mount Herzl, known as Har Zikaron (Mount of Remembrance), is Yad Vashem, Israel's national Holocaust memorial. At the mount's peak is the grave of Theodore Herzl, the founding father of modern Zionism. This provides a highly symbolic representation of modern Jewish history, that within three years of the lowest point in Jewish history, the Holocaust, the State of Israel was established.

Mount Herzl is the site of the annual official State ceremony marking the conclusion of Memorial Day for Israel's fallen and the commencement of Israel's Independence Day festivities.

For extra on these articles & more visit www.theus.org.uk/shabbatshalom

PARASHA QUIZ
BY ALIYA (CALL UP)

1. What did Jacob make Joseph promise before he died?

2. Which of Joseph's sons was born first?

3. Which grandson did Jacob bless with his right hand and why?

4. Which of Jacob's sons got the first blessing and why?

5. Who received the last two blessings and why?

6. Where was Jacob buried? With whom?

7. What did Joseph make the Children of Israel promise before he died?

Answers:

1. That he would not bury Jacob in Egypt, but rather in the Land of Canaan

2. Menashe

3. Ephraim. Even though he was the younger son, Jacob wanted to give him the greater blessing

4. Reuben, because he was the firstborn

5. Joseph and Benjamin, because they were the sons of Rachel, Jacob's beloved

6. The Cave of Machpela, with his wife Leah, his parents Isaac and Rebecca, and his grandparents Abraham and Sarah

7. To take his remains with them at the time of the Exodus

PERSONALITY OF THE WEEK
NATHANIEL MAYER ROTHSCHILD (1840–1915)

Nathaniel Mayer ("Natty"), the First Baron Rothschild, was the great-grandson of Mayer Amschel Rothschild, founder of the international banking family. His grandparents were amongst the earliest Ashkenazi Jews integrated into English society. Nathaniel studied at Trinity College Cambridge, becoming friends with the Prince of Wales, the future Edward VII.

He headed the NM Rothschild and Sons bank from 1879, funding the Suez Canal, Cecil Rhodes and De Beers as well as philanthropic housing schemes for London's poor Jews.

From 1865 to 1885 Nathaniel represented Aylesbury as a Liberal MP. He was a close friend of Disraeli through his father, Lionel, who had been the first observant Jewish Member able to take his seat in the House of Commons in 1858. In 1885 he was raised to the House of Lords by Gladstone and was its first practising Jewish member.

Nathaniel lent his name and considerable financial support to protests against pogroms and antisemitism in Russia. He was President of the United Synagogue from 1879 until his death, appointing Chief Rabbis Hermann Adler and Joseph Hertz. He was an active President of the Jews' Free School and Principal Warden of the Great Synagogue. The Board of Deputies would not make any important move without his approval.

He married Emma Louise (a cousin) in 1867 and had three children, Lionel Walter, Evelina and Nathaniel Charles. He was buried in Willesden Jewish Cemetery.

Rabbi Jeremy Lawrence

SHEMOT

**Anonymously dedicated
to the memory of soldiers
who fell defending
the State of Israel**

שְׁמוֹת

Shemot

1st SEDRA IN:

שְׁמוֹת

Shemot

BY NUMBERS:

124 verses
1,763 words
6,762 letters

HEADLINES:

The start of the slavery; introduction to Moses

Parasha Summary

Joseph's generation passes on. The new Pharaoh of Egypt makes the Israelites into slaves and orders their male children to be drowned in the River Nile. A Jewish woman places her baby (Moses) in a basket on the river to save him, where he is found by Pharaoh's daughter and raised in the palace. Moses sees injustice and, having killed an Egyptian, flees to Midian. Moses marries Zippora, the daughter of Midian's priest, and they have two sons. God calls Moses from a burning bush and instructs him to free the Israelites from Egypt. But Pharaoh makes life even harder for them.

THE NAME OF ISRAEL

When David Ben-Gurion declared statehood on 14 May 1948, the name of the new state was not obvious. Members of the early Zionist movement had usually referred to the hoped for nation as "the Jewish State," as it was called by Theodore Herzl: Der Judenstaat. During the British Mandate, *Eretz Yisrael* appeared in Hebrew (alongside 'Palestine' in English and Arabic) on the local currency, stamps and official documents, lending the name 'Israel' official status.

In the lead-up to 14 May, the Jewish leadership met in Tel Aviv to discuss names. According to *Palestine Post* writer Moshe Brilliant, at first the group wanted 'Judah', the name of the ancient Jewish Kingdom. But it was rejected as most of historic Judah fell outside the borders of the fledgling State according to the United Nations Partition Plan.

Other possibilities included 'Zion', but then someone suggested 'Israel'. A vote was held and 'Israel' won by 7 to 3. Brilliant suggested that Ben-Gurion chose the name, though Moshe Sharett, Israel's second Prime Minister, had been calling the future country 'The State of Israel' in speeches since at least 1946, while Ben-Gurion had used Medinat HaYehudim ('The State of the Jews'). But it was certainly Ben-Gurion who declared the name to the world later that week, bringing the State of Israel into reality.

For extra on these articles & more visit www.theus.org.uk/shabbatshalom

QUOTE OF THE WEEK

To really observe the Sabbath in our day and age! To cease for a whole day from all business, from all work, amidst the frenzied hurry-scurry of our age! To close the stock exchanges, the stores, the factories – how would it be possible? The pulse of life would stop beating and the world perish! The world perish? To the contrary, it would be saved.

Rabbi Samson Raphael Hirsch (1808–1888)

PERSONALITY OF THE WEEK
RABBI SAMSON RAPHAEL HIRSCH

Rabbi Samson Raphael Hirsch was an outstanding leader of German Jewry who was critical in framing the Orthodox Jewish response to modernity.

He was born in Hamburg on 20 June 1808, at a time when German Jewish practice was dominated by the 'Enlightenment', fuelled by Reform Judaism. In 1830 he was elected Chief Rabbi of Oldenberg, where he wrote *The Nineteen Letters*, an intellectual defence of traditional Judaism, which made a considerable impact in Jewish circles. Crucially it was written in German, the vernacular of those around him, many of whom had left Judaism.

Two years later Rabbi Hirsch published *Horeb*, his exposition of the 613 *mitzvot* (commandments). In 1851 he moved to Frankfurt where he served until his death in 1888. He established a Jewish school offering both Jewish and secular subjects. Its motto was a phrase from *Pirkei Avot* (Ethics of the Fathers): *Torah im* (with) *derech eretz*. He suggested that *derech eretz* referred to secular culture and so justified a broader curriculum than had ever previously been used – certainly by Eastern European Jews. He described his ideal of the 'Israel *mensch*', the Jew steeped in *Torah* values but also familiar with the best of secular culture. He advocated advanced education for girls, another idea that was way ahead of its time.

He was a fighter for Jewish rights, as well as an educator, writer and thinker. In Frankfurt, he saw that the Jewish community had largely departed from *Torah* ideals and was dominated by the Reform movement, so his synagogue broke away from the official community, becoming independent. He then persuaded the government to give his community official recognition since German law required a community to have such recognition.

Rabbi Hirsch left an immense legacy, demonstrating that engagement in the world was possible while staying connected to traditional *Torah* values.

Rabbi Stanley Coten

QUIZ: NAMES IN ISRAEL

1. The most popular name, the founder of the second largest religion in Israel today.

2. The second most popular name, Jacob's favourite son.

3. The most popular girls' name, meaning 'date tree'.

4. The most popular girls' name in Jerusalem, the first matriarch.

5. The most popular boys' name in Jerusalem, the most famous king of Israel.

6. The most popular boys' name in Tel Aviv, meaning 'my light'.

7. The most popular girls' name in Tel Aviv, meaning 'water' in Aramaic.

8. The most popular girls' name for Muslim Israelis, the name of Moses' sister.

Answers:
1. Muhammad
2. Yosef
3. Tamar
4. Sara
5. David
6. Ori
7. Maya
8. Miryam

SEDRA:

וָאֵרָא
Vaera

2nd SEDRA IN:
שְׁמוֹת
Shemot

BY NUMBERS:
121 verses
1,748 words
6,701 letters

HEADLINES:
Seven of the ten plagues

Parasha Summary

Despite God's message that they will be redeemed, the Israelites remain in terrible slavery. God again tells Moses and Aaron to deliver the Israelites from the land of Egypt. The genealogy of Reuben, Simeon, Levi and their descendants is recorded. Moses and Aaron, according to God's command, perform a miracle with a snake and tell Pharaoh God's message: to let the Israelites leave Egypt. But he refuses and the first seven plagues occur. After the seventh plague, God hardens Pharaoh's heart and he again refuses to let the Israelites go.

PERSONALITY OF THE WEEK: Chief Rabbi Nathan Marcus HaCohen Adler (1803–1890)

even by the aristocracy. In 1833, the Duchess of Cambridge was very ill and Rabbi Adler's congregation was asked to pray for her. After she recovered, the Duke sent Rabbi Adler his thanks and 100 gold Friedrichs. Rabbi Adler returned the money, asking for it to be given to the poor.

In 1845, British Jewry appointed Rabbi Adler as Chief Rabbi. His focus was on education, synagogues and charitable institutions. He also wrote numerous commentaries, responsa and translations of classic *Torah* works.

In 1866, amid friction and rivalry between five London synagogues – which even led to a body being left in the street until they agreed on who would pay for burial – Rabbi Adler successfully convinced the leaders to form the United Synagogue to ensure essential communal provisions.

Rabbi Daniel Sturgess

Chief Rabbi Adler is credited as the founder of the United Synagogue, as well as Jews' College, and of laying the foundations of the Chief Rabbinate as we know it today.

Born in Hanover, Germany, Rabbi Adler gained an extensive *Torah* education from his father, the Chief Rabbi of Hanover, and a broad secular education, studying classics and modern languages.

Rabbi Adler was well-respected in Hanover,

For extra on these articles & more visit www.theus.org.uk/shabbatshalom

PARASHA QUIZ

1. Why did Moses say he was unqualified to lead the Israelites out of Egypt?

2. What were Moses' mother and father called?

3. What was Aaron's wife called?

4. How much older than Moses was Aaron?

5. God told Moses He would harden Pharaoh's heart and Pharaoh would not let the Israelites go. Why did God say He was doing this?

6. After the fourth plague, Pharaoh told Moses and Aaron to take the people and sacrifice to God. They refused. Why?

7. Under which plague were the Jews and their flocks safe, as long as they were in Goshen?

STORY: THE ATTENBOROUGHS' DECISION

In 1939, the parents of Richard (later to be Lord) Attenborough who passed away in 2014, had offered refuge to a number of Jewish children escaping from Germany on the Kindertransport. Two Jewish girls staying with them were on their way to the United States, but when war was declared they were unable to cross the Atlantic.

The Attenboroughs wanted to offer the girls a home during the war, but felt it was a decision that could only be made as a family. Richard described how his parents called him and his two brothers together. They explained that Helga and Irene were Jewish, their parents had been sent to concentration camps and were unlikely to survive. The girls had no one to care for them and nowhere to go.

Lord Attenborough recalled his parents' words: 'We want to adopt the girls. We think it is the right thing to do. But we will only do it if you agree. It will call for sacrifices. We were a family of five. Now we will be a family of seven. There will be things we won't be able to afford. There will be things you will have to share. One of those will be love. You know how much we love you. But now you will have to share that love with Helga and Irene. We will have to show them special affection, because you have a family, but now they have no one at all.'

The boys agreed. Thinking back, Lord Attenborough described it as the most important day of his life. He had been given the chance to sacrifice something for someone else. He had been invited by his parents to join them in an act of courage and generosity.

Parasha Summary

Bo details the last three of the plagues and the institution of *Pesach*, both at the time of the Exodus itself and as it was subsequently to be celebrated. God sends the eighth and ninth plagues, locusts and darkness, but Pharaoh still refuses to free the Israelite slaves. God tells Moses that the tenth plague will kill all the firstborn Egyptians. God commands each Israelite family to slaughter a lamb and spread the blood on their doorposts in order to protect their firstborns. After the firstborns die, Pharaoh demands that the Israelites leave. The long exile was at an end. The Israelites had begun their journey to freedom. Several *mitzvot*, including *Tefillin* and teaching about the Exodus, are also referenced in *Bo*.

3rd SEDRA IN:

שְׁמוֹת
Shemot

BY NUMBERS:
106 verses
1,655 words
6,149 letters

HEADLINES:

Pesach and the Exodus

DVAR TORAH: Rosh Chodesh

The very first *mitzva* (commandment) given to the Jewish people, recorded in *Parashat Bo* as they prepared to leave Egypt, was to sanctify the start of each month. Today, we call this *Rosh Chodesh* (head of the month), which marks a new month in the Jewish calendar.

The timing for the giving of this commandment was very poignant. Having control over how to spend one's time is one of the most telling signs of freedom and it was especially powerful for Jews leaving slavery. Our ability to sanctify time, both how we spend it and through our Jewish calendar, is at the heart of Jewish life.

Nowadays on the *Shabbat* before *Rosh Chodesh*, known as *Shabbat Mevarachim* (the *Shabbat* of Blessing), we say prayers for the coming month, announcing its name and the day/s of the week on which *Rosh Chodesh* will occur. This marks when the 'rebirth' of the moon takes place – a monthly renaissance which Rabbi Eliyahu Munk (1900–1981) in his book, *World of Prayer*, suggests is the guarantee, permanently written into natural law as it were, that Israel too will ever be reborn.

On *Rosh Chodesh* we recite festive *Hallel* prayers, the *Musaf* service and a *Torah* reading describing the offerings brought in the Temple on *Rosh Chodesh*. We also add the *Ya'aleh Veyavo* paragraph to the *Amida* and *Bensching* (Grace after meals). Some people also eat or wear something special on *Rosh Chodesh*. It's a good chance to reflect on how we spend our time, as well as the freedoms given to our ancestors in Egypt.

Rabbi Nicky Liss

For extra on these articles & more visit www.theus.org.uk/shabbatshalom

QUOTE OF THE WEEK

I wish there was... kind of a worldwide day where we're not on our phones - like a movement. I just think something like this would be really great for our minds, especially because kids today - if they weren't born in the 80s - don't even know what a life without internet is like. And I think it's going to be really difficult for our focus and our attention spans moving forward. So I'd love if the world implemented an actual day of real rest.

Katy Perry

QUIZ: A HISTORY OF THE JEWS IN BRITAIN

1. The first written record of Jews in England dates back to the time of William the Conqueror in which century?

2. Which king expelled the Jews from England in 1290?

3. When were Jews readmitted to England by Oliver Cromwell?

4. Which representative body of the Jewish community was established in 1760?

5. Who was the first Jew to be knighted, by Queen Victoria, in 1837?

6. Which communities are the furthest north and west in mainland Britain?

7. In 1858, after the legal emancipation of the Jews in Britain, and the law restricting the oath of office to Christians was changed, where was Lionel de Rothschild finally able to take up office?

8. Which Israeli President was born in the UK and where?

9. What is the largest union of British synagogues to this day, founded in 1870?

10. Approximately how many Jews live in Britain today?

JEWISH HISTORY

On 4 February 1657, Oliver Cromwell gave Antonio Fernandez Carvajal, a Portuguese-Jewish merchant living as a hidden Jew in England, the assurance of the right of Jews to remain in England. This unofficially ended the ban on Jews living in England and paved the way for the rebirth of the Jewish community in England.

Answers:
1. 11th century (1070)
2. Edward I
3. 1657
4. The Board of Deputies of British Jews
5. Sir Moses Montefiore
6. Aberdeen & Swansea
7. House of Commons as a Member of Parliament
8. Chaim Hertzog, Belfast
9. The United Synagogue
10. 290,000

4th SEDRA IN:

שְׁמוֹת
Shemot

BY NUMBERS:
116 verses
1,681 words
6,423 letters

HEADLINES:
Crossing of
and the Song
at the Sea

Parasha Summary

The Israelites leave Egypt and God deliberately leads them on a circuitous route. God tells Moses that the Israelites should camp at the Sea of Reeds, but then Pharaoh changes his mind about freeing the Israelites and chases them with horses and chariots. With the Egyptians on their tail, the people come close to despair. Then, in one of the supreme miracles of history, God splits the sea and Moses leads the Israelites through. When the Egyptians enter, God closes the waters and the Egyptians drown. The Israelites then sing a momentous song of faith and deliverance. But their troubles are not over. The Israelites begin to complain about life in the desert as they lack water and food. God sends oasis springs and then water from a rock, and manna from heaven. *Beshalach* ends as it began, with the prospect of war, this time against the Amalekites, who cowardly attack the weaker Israelites towards the rear of the Israelite column. Joshua, at Moses' command, leads men to repel the Amalekites whose actions are also an attack against God.

DVAR TORAH:
Tu B'Shvat, the Environment and Judaism

Tu B'Shvat literally means, the fifteenth of the Hebrew month of Shvat. The significance of the date derives from a dispute in the *Mishna* between the academies of Hillel and Shammai, who argue about the annual date of the new year for trees. When they say 'new year', they do not mean a celebration. Rather, they mean the concept of tithing the produce of trees and when the start and end of the tithing year should be – in essence, a consideration of the tithing year of tree produce. The academy of Shammai said the year begins on 1 Shvat, Hillel said 15 Shvat. Since the normative law is decided according to the academy of Hillel, 15 Shvat became the beginning of the tithing year for fruit of the tree.

Tu B'Shvat enables us to focus on an important message: we do not own nature and we cannot fully empty nature of its bounty simply for our own benefit. In an age where productivity and demand have massively increased due to growing technological ability, we have become used – at least in the developed world – to fulfilling our desires for food and are less aware of what this does to nature itself. Early in the *Torah*, Adam was placed in the Garden of Eden "to work it and conserve it". *Tu B'Shvat* allows us to connect to both the working of nature, and conserving it.

Rabbi David Mason

For extra on these articles & more visit www.theus.org.uk/shabbatshalom

JEWISH HISTORY
NATAN SHARANSKY'S RELEASE FROM PRISON

Natan Sharansky was born in the Soviet Union in 1948, the year the State of Israel was established. He excelled in physics and chess. But at that time in the Soviet Union, Jews were forbidden to practise Judaism or study Hebrew. As a passionate Jew and Zionist, Sharansky taught himself Hebrew and learnt about Israel, inspiring others to follow his lead.

During the early 1970s, despite great danger, tens of thousands of Soviet Jews applied for exit visas to Israel. The Soviet authorities saw this as a serious challenge and acted to stop the Jewish exodus. Public trials were held against Zionists expressing a desire to leave, and Jews applying for visas suffered severe consequences.

In 1973, Sharansky applied for a visa to Israel. His application was denied, as authorities falsely claimed that he had been given access to information vital to national security. Sharansky decided to represent other Jews who were refused visas to Israel, called 'refuseniks', and make the world aware of their brutal persecution at the hands of the Soviet authorities.

Sharansky was arrested in 1977, accused of providing the West with lists of refuseniks. He was sentenced to 13 years of forced labour. In an attempt to break Sharansky's Jewish and Zionist spirit, he was incarcerated in solitary confinement for long periods – but instead he used this time to learn and practise Hebrew despite being kept in dreadful conditions.

As a result of an international campaign led by his wife, Avital, Sharansky was released on 11 February 1986. He finally accomplished his life-long dream and went straight to his new life in Israel.

Rabbi Cobi Ebrahimoff

QUOTE OF THE WEEK

They tried their best to find a place where I was isolated. But all the resources of a superpower cannot isolate the man who hears a voice of freedom, a voice I heard from the very chamber of my soul.

Natan Sharansky

DISCUSSION QUESTIONS

1. Why do you think that Natan Sharansky was so determined to preserve his Judaism and reach Israel, despite being persecuted by the Soviets for doing so?

2. What lessons can Jews today learn from Natan and Avital Sharansky and the other refuseniks?

Parasha Summary

Yitro can be divided into two parts. First Moses tells his father-in-law, Yitro, about the miracle of the Exodus. Yitro proclaims that the Israelite God is greater than all other deities and he brings an offering to God. Yitro then advises Moses to delegate leadership roles, in order not to tire himself out. This is Israel's first system of governance – leaders of thousands, hundreds, fifties and tens. In the second part, the Israelites camp at the bottom of Mount Sinai. After three days, the mountain fills with smoke and God delivers the Ten Commandments and other *mitzvot* to His people during the Revelation at Sinai. This is *Matan Torah*, the giving of the *Torah*, the eternal constitution of the Jewish people, the Covenant between God and the Jewish people.

5th SEDRA IN:

שְׁמוֹת

Shemot

BY NUMBERS:

75 verses
1,105 words
4,022 letters

HEADLINES:

Giving of the Torah including the Ten Commandments

JEWISH HISTORY
DOÑA GRACIA

In a 16th century that produced famous and powerful women including Elizabeth I and Catherine of Medici, Doña Gracia stands out; her heroism, loyalty and faith easily eclipsing any epic legend.

Widowed at the age of 26, and forced for many years to live a dangerous double-life: outwardly a Catholic, secretly a Jewess, she dined with the most powerful rulers of her day, including Queen Maria of Habsburg, Maximillian II and the Sultan of Turkey. She also oversaw a financial empire, whilst clandestinely providing sanctuary for thousands of Marrano (secret) Jews.

She faced imprisonment and death on numerous occasions for her beliefs but managed to thwart the all-powerful Inquisition and defy her enemies. Doña Gracia was one of the most outstanding figures in Jewish history, yet amazing is virtually unknown.

Doña Gracia could have lived a fairytale existence, surrounded by the princes of Europe, but opted instead for the more difficult and often dangerous route: living for and by the truth. In our 21st-century democracies, we would do well to reflect on her courage and integrity and her absolute commitment to her People, her Judaism and her Land. She was truly a Jewish heroine.

Extract from 'Doña Gracia: An Inspiring Example', 60 Days for 60 Years Israel, (2008) Rabbi Aubrey Hersh

PERSONALITY OF THE WEEK
SIR MOSES MONTEFIORE

Sir Moses Montefiore was a highly successful businessman, Sheriff of the City of London and a personal friend of Queen Victoria. He was dedicated to the care and wellbeing of his people.

Despite his growing fame and fortune, Sir Moses did not assimilate. On the contrary, he became ever more engaged with Judaism and the Jewish people. He headed the Board of Deputies of British Jews for close to 30 years and he drew on his personal connections with heads of state such as the Pope, the Sultan and the Tsar of Russia to curtail antisemitic attacks.

Sir Moses said that his fortune did not consist of the money he banked, but that which he distributed to charity. Therefore, on his seven trips to the Land of Israel, he handed out vast sums to alleviate poverty and promote Jewish learning. His windmill still stands as testimony to his efforts to ensure the wellbeing of the Jews of Jerusalem.

Rabbi Gideon Sylvester

DISCUSSION QUESTIONS

1. What leadership values did Sir Moses display?

2. Did Sir Moses celebrate or hide his Judaism? Why do you think this?

3. Have you been to the windmill in Jerusalem? What does it represent to you?

SHABBAT QUIZ: FOOD

1. What is the bread eaten at *Shabbat* meals traditionally called?

2. What are the prime ingredients of *cholent*?

3. Why is *cholent* a classic *Shabbat* food?

4. What is *kiddush* made over on Friday night?

5. What does *kugel* mean in German?

6. How many meals do we have during *Shabbat*?

7. Do *Shabbat* meals have to include meat?

Answers:
1. *Challa*
2. Beans, barley, potatoes and meat.
3. Cooking is forbidden on *Shabbat*. *Cholent* (a slow-cooked dish) can be put on the heat before *Shabbat* and eaten hot on *Shabbat* day
4. Kosher wine or grape juice
5. Ball
6. Three
7. No

Parasha Summary

Following the giving of the *Torah* at Mount Sinai, *Mishpatim* expands on the laws of the *Torah*, starting to cover civil and criminal laws as well as laws about our relationship with God. The *parasha* includes laws about the prohibition to worship other deities, *kashrut*, business ethics, treatment of animals, slaves and their release, personal injuries and property, social responsibility, justice and compassion. God also outlines the three Biblical festivals which will ultimately include an obligation to go to the Temple in Jerusalem: *Pesach*, *Shavuot* and *Sukkot*. God provides an angel to protect the Israelites from their enemies and warns them not to worship other gods. *Mishpatim* ends with further details of the Revelation and giving of the *Torah*, detailing how Moses ascended Mount Sinai to learn from God for 40 days and 40 nights, leaving Aaron and Chur to look after the people in Moses's absence. The famous phrase *Naaseh venishma*, 'We will do and [then] listen', appears in *Mishpatim*.

6th SEDRA IN:

שְׁמוֹת

Shemot

BY NUMBERS:

118 verses
1,462 words
5,313 letters

HEADLINES:

Civil laws,
Yom Tov,
Revelation

PERSONALITY OF THE WEEK
BENJAMIN DISRAELI (1804–1881)

Benjamin Disraeli was born Jewish and is considered Britain's first Jewish Prime Minister, even though he was a practising Anglican. In 1813, Disraeli's father, Isaac Disraeli, quarrelled with the leadership of the Bevis Marks Synagogue in the City of London. This quarrel led Isaac to have his children, including Benjamin, baptised as Anglicans in 1817. Until 1858 Jews were excluded from Parliament so, if not for his father's decision, Disraeli's political career could never have taken the form it did.

Benjamin Disraeli was born in London on 21 December 1804. Disraeli trained as a solicitor and, like his father, he took a keen interest in literature. His first novel, Vivian Grey, was published in 1826. It sold well and was followed by several others.

Disraeli was also interested in politics. In the early 1830s he stood in several elections as a Whig, Radical and Independent, each time unsuccessfully. He was eventually elected to

represent Maidstone in 1837, but his maiden speech in the House of Commons was poorly received. After enduring a great deal of barracking, he ended: "Though I sit down now, the time will come when you will hear me."

In 1868, Lord Derby resigned and Disraeli briefly became Prime Minister, before losing that year's general election. He returned to opposition until the general election of 1874, when he led the Tories as they won an outright majority.

Disraeli got on very well with Queen Victoria, who approved of Disraeli's imperialist views and his desire to make Britain the most powerful nation in the world. In 1876 Victoria agreed to his suggestion that she should accept the title of Empress of India.

In August 1876 Queen Victoria granted Disraeli the title Lord Beaconsfield. He left the House of Commons but continued as Prime Minister in the House of Lords. In 1878 he gained great acclaim for his success in limiting Russia's power in the Balkans.

The Liberals defeated the Conservatives in the 1880 General Election and Disraeli decided to retire from politics. Disraeli hoped to spend his retirement writing novels but died the following year. Disraeli neither changed his obviously Jewish name nor denied his origins, even when the victim of antisemitic jibes.

For extra on these articles & more visit www.theus.org.uk/shabbatshalom

QUOTE OF THE WEEK

In 1835, Daniel O'Connell attacked Disraeli in the House of Commons. In the course of his unrestrained invective, he referred to Disraeli's Jewish ancestry. Disraeli replied, "Yes, I am a Jew, and while the ancestors of the Right Honourable gentleman were brutal savages in an unknown island, mine were priests in the temple of Solomon."

Benjamin Disraeli

QUIZ: INFLUENTIAL JEWISH LEADERS

1. Greatest Jewish prophet of all time
2. His sister, a prophetess
3. Great Jewish king who made Jerusalem the capital
4. Great medieval rabbi, philosopher and doctor
5. Founder of the Beis Yaakov Schools network
6. Biblical king who built the First Temple
7. Rabbi who compiled the *Mishna*
8. A great Jewish storyteller, film-maker and founder of the Shoah Visual History Foundation

Answers:
1. Moses
2. Miriam
3. King David
4. Rambam
5. Sarah Schneirer
6. King Solomon
7. Rabbi Yehuda HaNasi
8. Steven Spielberg

JEWISH HISTORY
TECHNION UNIVERSITY

On 22 February 1914, the Technion University was under construction in Haifa. The Board of Trustees made the momentous decision to reverse its vote of October 1913 for German to be the language of instruction, and decided that Hebrew should be spoken instead. This was a vital moment in the development of the Zionist enterprise in the Land of Israel.

DISCUSSION QUESTIONS

1. Do you learn Hebrew? Why?
2. Do you think speaking Hebrew is an important value? Why?
3. Does Hebrew belong more in the *Beit Knesset* (synagogue) and the *Beit Midrash* (study hall), or in the university and the street?

Parasha Summary

God commands the Children of Israel to donate *terumah* (a gift) for the building of the *Mishkan* (Tabernacle), so that God may "dwell among them". The *Mishkan* is a kind of portable Temple, which the Israelites used in the desert prior to the construction of the Temple in Jerusalem. God gives precise instructions for the construction of the ark, table and *menorah*, as well as the other items in the *Mishkan*. God also gives directions about how to construct the *Mishkan* itself.

7th SEDRA IN:

שְׁמוֹת

Shemot

BY NUMBERS:

96 verses
1,145 words
4,692 letters

HEADLINES:

Instructions to build the Mishkan

QUOTE OF THE WEEK

Jews contributed to the world some of its most transformative ideas. It's worth listening to the testimony of non-Jewish writers on this subject. Here, for instance, is the Catholic historian Paul Johnson: "To the Jews we owe the idea of equality before the law, both divine and human; of the sanctity of life and the dignity of the human person; of the individual conscience and so of personal redemption; of the collective conscience and so of social responsibility; of peace as an abstract ideal and love as the foundation of justice, and many other items which constitute the basic moral furniture of the human mind."

Another Catholic historian, Thomas Cahill, wrote this in his book *The Gifts of the Jews* : "The Jews gave us the Outside and the Inside – our outlook and our inner life. We can hardly get up in the morning or cross the street without being Jewish. We dream Jewish dreams and hope Jewish hopes. Most of our best words, in fact – new, adventure, surprise; unique, individual, person, vocation; time, history, future; freedom, progress, spirit; faith, hope, justice – are the gifts of the Jews."…

… Judaism has always believed in the power of ideas, and it remains the only non-violent way to change the world.

Extracts from Rabbi Jonathan Sacks, Introduction to *Covenant & Conversation* 5778 (www.rabbisacks.org)

QUIZ: FORBIDDEN MELACHA

1. How many categories of *melacha* (creative labour used in the *Mishkan*) are there on *Shabbat*?

2. What were these *melachot* used for in the *Mishkan*: sowing, reaping, grinding and baking?

3. What were these *melachot* used for in the *Mishkan*: shearing wool, dyeing, spinning, tying a knot?

4. What were these *melachot* used for in the *Mishkan*: slaughtering, skinning, tanning, cutting?

5. What were these *melachot* used for in the *Mishkan*: building, breaking down?

Answers:
1. 39
2. Baking bread
3. Making curtains out of material
4. Making curtains out of leather
5. Assembling and dismantling the Mishkan

PERSONALITY OF THE WEEK
DAYAN YECHEZKEL ABRAMSKY (1886–1976)

The Jewish community in Dashkovichy, Lithuania, was so small that it did not always have enough men for a *minyan*, yet it raised a scholar of the calibre of Rabbi Yechezkel Abramsky.

His scholarship and bravery saw him become a leading opponent of Soviet attempts to eradicate Judaism following the Russian Revolution of 1917. The Soviet authorities twice blocked him from assuming the rabbinate of Petach Tivka in Mandatory Palestine and closed down a *Torah* magazine that he had founded. In 1929, Rabbi Abramsky was arrested and sentenced to five years' hard labour in the brutal conditions of Siberia. Even there, he did not stop studying and teaching, even writing study notes on discarded pieces of paper that he found.

An international campaign to free him, including interventions by both the UK and Germany, succeeded in 1931, when Rabbi Abramsky was released and came to London. In 1934, Chief Rabbi Hertz appointed Rabbi Abramsky as the senior dayan (judge) of the London Beth Din rabbinic court. His scholarship and piety established Beth Din procedures that continue to this day.

In 1951, he retired to Jerusalem where he continued his scholarship and activism. In 1956, he was awarded the prestigious Israel Prize, for rabbinic literature. His funeral in 1976 was attended by tens of thousands of people.

A STORY FOR SHABBAT

Once a king wanted to discover the sweetest music in the world. He brought together all the musicians in his kingdom and listened to each play their instrument one at a time. But no single melody stood out to him as the sweetest. Then he asked all the musicians to play at once, but the noise was almost unbearable. Finally an elderly woman came forward and set two candles down in front of the king. He demanded silence as he watched the woman say the blessing on the candles and welcome in the *Shabbat* Queen. The king asked for the meaning of her actions, and she explained that the sweetest music of all is the sound of the rest and peace of *Shabbat*.

ESTHER CAILINGOLD

Esther Cailingold was born in Whitechapel, London, in 1925. She attended North London Collegiate School and London University and was active in Bnei Akiva. Deeply religious and Zionist, in 1946 she accepted a position teaching English and History at the Evelina de Rothschild School in Jerusalem. In the spring of 1948, she volunteered to assist with the hazardous defence of the Jewish Quarter of the Old City of Jerusalem as Jordanian Legionnaires closed in. By 18 May there was nothing left to fight with.

Most of the defenders were dead or injured. Tragically, whilst displaying immense bravery, Esther Cailingold also lay mortally wounded. On the day the white flag was raised she died.

Esther Cailingold is buried in the military cemetery on Mount Herzl, Jerusalem. She was twenty-two. Her sister Mimi later became my wife, and her brother, Asher, one of my dearest friends.

(Adapted from *The Prime Ministers*, Yehuda Avner, The Toby Press 2010)

8th SEDRA IN:

שְׁמוֹת

Shemot

BY NUMBERS:
101 verses
1,412 words
5,430 letters

HEADLINES:
Instructions for
Cohanim and
the Mishkan

Parasha Summary

In *Tetzaveh*, the role of the priests in the service of the *Mishkan* (Tabernacle) takes centre stage. God appoints Aaron as High Priest and his sons as regular priests (*cohanim*). The first *mitzva* (command) for the *cohanim* is the daily kindling of the *menorah* with olive oil. God describes the priestly clothing and explains how to properly inaugurate the priests. A *Tamid* (daily) offering is to be brought in the morning and afternoon (which are paralleled in our morning and afternoon prayer services). An incense altar is also constructed.

DVAR TORAH

Tetzaveh, with its focus on the special garments of the *Cohanim* (priests) in the *Mishkan* and Temple, emphasises the greatness that humans can attain.

Subsequent to his creation, the *Torah* tells us "Adam assigned names to all the creatures..." The *Midrash* (Rabbinic exegesis) notes that despite God's request to the angels to assign names to all the creatures, they were unable to do so. It was then that God requested Adam to name them.

In Hebrew, the assignment of a name defines its very essence. The name assigned for humanity was 'Adam', since Adam was created from *adama* (the earth). But why was Adam named after the mundane, lowly earth?

I read a beautiful explanation for this. Earth by itself has only latent potential for growth. A seed that is nurtured after planting can grow and develop into a tree that produces fruit. So it is with humanity. We are all born with tremendous potential to accomplish and achieve great things with God's help. Whether that potential comes to fruition like the soil is in large measure dependent on our willingness to invest the time and effort necessary to succeed.

The *Cohanim* were people of tremendous spiritual potential. Their proper service in the sanctuaries, trained by Moses and Aaron, helped them to rise to spiritual greatness, something which we can all emulate to fulfil our own potential.

Rabbi Pinchas Hackenbroch

For extra on these articles & more visit www.theus.org.uk/shabbatshalom

THE EMBLEM OF THE STATE OF ISRAEL

The official state emblem of the State of Israel is a *menorah* (based on the *menorah* found on the Arch of Titus in Rome, which depicts the exiles carrying away the vessels from the Second Temple). It is flanked by an olive branch on each side, with *Yisrael*, the Hebrew word for Israel, underneath. The design was the winning entry in a design competition in 1948, created by Gabriel and Maxim Shamir. The *menorah* represents how Israel must provide 'light' (benefit) to the world, as the Temple did, and the olive branches represent peace.

QUIZ

1. In which Biblical structures was the *menorah* lit?

2. Who donated the large *menorah* which stands near Israel's *Knesset* (parliament building)?

3. True or false? Olives are one of the fruits for which the Land of Israel is praised by the *Torah*.

4. Why were blue and white chosen as the official colours of the State of Israel's flag and emblem?

Answers:
1. The *Mishkan* (portable Sanctuary) and the *Beit Mikdash* (Temple)
2. Members of the British Labour Party, on 15 April 1956
3. True
4. To match the white and *techelet* (a form of blue) colours of *tzitzit*

DISCUSSION QUESTIONS

1. What contrasts can you suggest between the Arch of Titus and the emblem of the State of Israel?

2. Why do you think the *menorah* was chosen for the emblem?

3. Why do you think the olive branches were chosen?

Shabbat Kiddush

Shabbat is a day of holiness. How do we celebrate this holiness? In our home, we have special *Shabbat* treats, enjoy *kiddush* wine and serve our most delicious foods. This is the Jewish approach to pleasure – talking the physical and making it spiritual by using it for holy tasks, like the pleasure of *Shabbat*.

Yet later on in the *Torah* (*Bemidbar*, chapter 6) we learn of the *Nazir*, who vows to abstain from wine or any grape derivatives for a period of time. This abstention seems to be to avoid sinning through wine and, though the *Nazir* is praised for this piety, he needs to bring a sin offering after his time as a *Nazir* concludes. But what was his sin?

The great scholar Maimonides (Rambam, 1135–1204) explains that the problem was that the *Nazir* elected to abstain from a physical pleasure, which the *Torah* permits. *Kiddush* over wine or grape juice is central to *Shabbat* and *Yom Tov*. The word *kiddush* even means 'holiness', showing how we use the grapes for a sacred rather than a drunken purpose. From this perspective, holiness would seem to be gained by self-control and effective management of our behaviour, while enjoying the world we live in. *Kiddush* on *Shabbat* and *Yom Tov* regularly reminds us of this.

Rebbetzen Jacqueline Feldman

Parasha Summary

Moses takes a census of the Children of Israel and collects a half-*shekel* from males over 20. The Israelites are instructed to keep *Shabbat*.

Moses is on Mount Sinai. God gives him the two tablets of stone, but meanwhile the Israelites build a Golden Calf. God is angry, but Moses successfully argues for Divine forgiveness and is taught prayers for mercy which we still recite today, especially on *Yom Kippur*. He breaks the tablets when he sees the idolatrous calf, but later goes up Mount Sinai for another 40 days to receive a second set. Other laws, including those about the festivals, are also given.

9th SEDRA IN:

שְׁמוֹת

Shemot

BY NUMBERS:

139 verses
2,002 words
7,424 letters

HEADLINES:

The Golden Calf and aftermath

Shabbat Candles – The Beracha

In general, and with very few exceptions, the *beracha* for a *mitzva* is recited prior to the fulfilment of the *mitzva*. Accordingly, many rabbinic authorities rule that even when lighting the *Shabbat* candles the *beracha* should be said before the candles are lit. They maintain that even if lighting the candles indicates an implicit acceptance of the sanctity of *Shabbat*, that does not happen until the candles have actually been lit. Sephardi practice is in accordance with this view.

However, Ashkenazi practice is to recite the *beracha* after lighting the candles, in deference to a minority rabbinic view that reciting the *beracha* is tantamount to inaugurating *Shabbat*. According to this opinion, were the *beracha* to be recited first, it would no longer be permissible to light the candles since *Shabbat* would have already commenced. In order to conform with the general rule that *berachot* should be said before the *mitzva* is done, recommended practice is that the person lighting the candles should cover his or her eyes before saying the *beracha*, so as not to benefit from the light until afterwards.

On *Yom Tov* a flame may be transferred and candles can be lit from an existing light. Consequently, most rabbinic authorities advise that when lighting the *Yom Tov* candles, the *beracha* should be recited after transferring the flame (which according to Ashkenazi practice cannot be done after saying the *beracha*), but before lighting the candles (which can be done even on *Yom Tov* proper). However, other rabbinic authorities recommend not deviating from normal Friday-night practice.

Rabbi Daniel Roselaar

For extra on these articles & more visit www.theus.org.uk/shabbatshalom

PERSONALITY OF THE WEEK
CHIEF RABBI SIR ISRAEL BRODIE

In *Parashat Bo*, the Jewish people finally experience the emancipation and liberation from the furnace of Egypt. The stewardship of Chief Rabbi Brodie, likewise, represented a period of huge transformation within British Jewry, following the atrocities of the decimation of European Jewry and the rebirth that ensued with the establishment of the State of Israel.

Chief Rabbi Brodie himself had served as an Army Chaplain in both World Wars, and was evacuated from Dunkirk in 1940. His appointment as Chief Rabbi of Great Britain and the Commonwealth in 1948 almost coincided with the founding of the State of Israel and it was he who composed the 'Prayer for the State of Israel' commonly recited in our synagogues. At the centenary celebration of the Board of Jewish Religious Education, he recalled his visit to a certain concentration camp after War World Two. The survivors had nowhere to go and had remained in the camp, and so passed the time by learning Modern Hebrew. As they gathered around the blackboard on the parade ground, he could see they were learning the future tense in the 'Holy Tongue'. On it was written: 'I will go to Israel. You will go to Israel. He will go to Israel' – a beautiful message of hope and revival.

Due to the influx of refugees from Europe, the landscape of British Jewry had vastly changed and there was a need

for a leader who had the stature, elocution and diplomacy to meet the needs of all, while resolutely preserving Orthodox values.

He passed away in 1979 and was described by his colleague, Rabbi Raymond Apple (www.oztorah.org), as a "gentleman, an ambassador, a remarkable speaker and an ornament to Judaism and Jewry."

Rabbi Meir Shindler

A STORY FOR SHABBAT

The Olympic Games in Rio de Janeiro opened on Friday night, 5th August 2016. Politicians from all over the world were present. There was one notable exception. Miri Regev, Israel's Culture and Sport Minister, did not attend as doing so would have necessitated her driving on *Shabbat*.

Even though she did not claim to be personally observant, she said that "*Shabbat*, our national day of rest, is one of the most important gifts that the Jewish people have given to the culture of humanity. As the representative of the State of Israel, the sole Jewish state on the planet, I unfortunately cannot take part in the opening ceremony of the Olympics because it would require me to break the holy Sabbath."

DISCUSSION QUESTIONS

1. Why did Miri Regev decide *Shabbat* observance was so important?

2. Baroness Altmann, who served in Prime Minister David Cameron's Cabinet, is probably the only *Shabbat*-observant Jew to have served in a British Cabinet. How can a Jewish politician in the UK make you proud to be Jewish?

Parasha Summary

Moses gathers the nation, instructs them to keep *Shabbat* and tells them of God's command to volunteer materials needed for the construction of the *Mishkan* (Tabernacle) and the priestly garments. Moses announces the appointment of the wise-hearted Bezalel and Ohaliab to oversee the construction, assisted by able craftsmen. When they collect all the donations, there is a surplus, so Moses tells the Israelites not to bring any more.

Betzalel starts work on the numerous items required for the *Mishkan*, including the *aron* (ark) with two cherubs on top; the *menorah* hammered from one piece of pure gold, and the *mizbe'ach* (altar) along with its anointing oil and incense spices.

DVAR TORAH: Art and faith

In *Vayakhel* we encounter Bezalel, who becomes the symbol of the artist in Judaism. Bezalel, with Ohaliab, makes the *Mishkan* (Tabernacle) and its furnishings, using his skills for the greater glory of God.

Although the aesthetic dimension of Judaism is often downplayed because of our discomfort with the physical imagery (which often led to idol worship), it is not wholly missing. There are visible symbols, like *tzitzit* and *mezuza*, and a "meta-*mitzva*" known as *hiddur mitzva* – 'beautifying the command'. In the *Mishkan* itself, its framework, furniture and the priests' clothes are "for dignity and beauty" (Exodus 28:2).

Omanut (art) has a semantic connection with emunah (faith), while the name Bezalel means "in the shadow of God". Art is the shadow cast by the radiance of God that suffuses all things. When art lets us see the wonder of creation as God's work and the human person as God's image, it becomes a powerful part of religious life. Art adds wonder to faith.

ART ADDS WONDER TO FAITH

Rabbi Jonathan Sacks, *Covenant And Conversation*, Vayakhel, 2011

PERSONALITY OF THE WEEK
DAVID BEN-GURION (1886–1973)

David Ben-Gurion was not only the first Prime Minister of the State of Israel, but was a leader of the Jewish community in *Eretz Yisrael* even before there was a State. Born in Poland, he made *aliya* aged 20. He immediately took on leadership roles in the Zionist community and became head of the Jewish Agency (effectively the pre-State government) in 1935, including the Hagana, the community's defence force.

On 14 May 1948, Ben-Gurion declared independence and the State of Israel was born. He became the de-facto Prime Minister and won its first election in February 1949. He served in this role until 1963 (taking a short break in 1954), guiding Israel through its earliest historic events.

Ben-Gurion was famous for his love of books, Bible study and the Negev desert. Thousands of people visit his simple home (and very large library!) in Kibbutz Sde Boker in the Negev every year.

For extra on these articles & more visit www.theus.org.uk/shabbatshalom

QUOTE OF THE WEEK

Shabbat is about family togetherness, personal growth and development... rather than enabling our fast-moving, sophisticated world and electronic equipment to dominate us.

CHIEF RABBI MIRVIS

A STORY FOR SHABBAT

A fortune-teller once told a non-Jew he would lose all his wealth to Yosef, a man well known for honouring *Shabbat*. To protect his riches, the non-Jew sold everything he owned and with the money bought a precious pearl, which he placed in the hat he always wore.

One Friday, as he was crossing a river, the wind blew his hat into the water and a fish swallowed the pearl. Just as the sun was setting, the fish was caught – but the fisherman wondered who would buy it so late in the day? People said to him, "Take it to Yosef. He always buys the tastiest food for *Shabbat*." Yosef bought the fish for his *Shabbat* meal, and while preparing it he found the pearl. They said about Yosef, "Whoever gives to *Shabbat*, *Shabbat* repays him!"

Talmud (Shabbat 119a)

ISRAEL
BEZALEL ACADEMY OF ARTS AND DESIGN

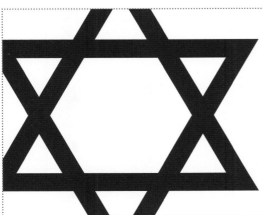

Did you know that Israel's world-famous national art school is named after Bezalel in our *parasha*?

The Bezalel Academy was founded in Jerusalem in 1906 by Boris Schatz, a painter who made *aliya* (moved to Israel) from Lithuania. This makes it one of Israel's oldest institutions of higher learning! Over the years Bezalel developed its own unique art movement, presenting Biblical and Zionist subjects in traditional European, Persian and Syrian styles – reflecting the mix of cultures in Israel. Today Bezalel has over 1500 students.

11th SEDRA IN:

שְׁמוֹת
Shemot

BY NUMBERS:
92 verses
1,182 words
4,432 letters

HEADLINES:
The Mishkan
and the
Cohanim

Parasha Summary

This is the final *parasha* in the book of *Shemot* – although the story continues! Moses does some bookkeeping, recording all the donations given towards the *Mishkan* (Tabernacle) and how they were used. The priestly garments are also detailed. The *Mishkan* is finally completed, Moses assembles it and God rests His presence there.

DVAR TORAH

There are four *mitzvot* (commandments) of *Purim*: hearing the *Purim* story (*megilla*), giving charity to the poor to fund their festive meal (*matanot la'evyonim*), giving two food items to a friend (*mishloach manot*) and having a festive meal (*seuda*). We can understand why we hear the *megilla* each year – but why do the other three all pertain to materialistic pleasure!

It seems that this emphasis on nurturing our bodies ironically captures the essence of the day.

Throughout the Bible, Jews are referred to as *Bnei Yisrael* or *Am Yisrael* (Children/People of Israel), but in the Book of Esther we are called *Yehudim* (Jews). This reflects what Haman wanted to destroy. There are two types of antisemitism: that which aims to destroy our faith; and that which aims to destroy any Jew, regardless of belief. Haman wanted the latter. Therefore on *Purim* we celebrate the infinite endurance of 'the Jew' – our simple existence, before any consideration of faith or practice.

The festivals do not sit in a vacuum; they flow into one another. The *Shulchan Aruch* (Code of Jewish Law) states that 30 days before a festival, we begin to prepare for it. Thirty days after *Purim* is *Pesach*, the celebration of our spiritual freedom. We can only contemplate our spiritual purpose in the world once we have celebrated our fundamental existence.

Rebbetzen Lauren Levin

PERSONALITY OF THE WEEK
THE MAHARAL OF PRAGUE

Rabbi Yehuda Loew, (1512-1609), known by the acronym 'Maharal', was one of the most influential rabbinic scholars of his time. He was the rabbi of Prague and an expert in science, philosophy and *kabbala*. His works are still widely studied.

He wrote commentaries on *agadata*, the non-legalistic texts of the *Talmud*, on *Pirkei Avot*, on many of the *Chagim* as well as a seminal work on the Rashi's commentary of the *Torah*, *Gur Aryeh*.

The Maharal is also the subject of what is understood by some scholars to be a 19th century legend about the creation of a *golem*, a creature made out of clay to defend the Jews of Prague from antisemitic attacks. This legend attests to the renown in which the Maharal continued to be held even after his passing.

Amongst his outstanding students were the authors of the *Tosafot Yom Tov* and *K'li Yakar* commentaries on the *Mishna* and *Torah* respectively.

His prominent descendants included Rabbi Nachman of Breslov and the *Baal Tanya*, the founder of *Chabad chassidut*. The famous Old-New Synagogue in Prague, where the Maharal served as rabbi, remains in active use today.

Rabbi David Rose

ONEG SHABBAT

We have a special *mitzva* (commandment) to enjoy *Shabbat*. The prophet Isaiah (58:13–14) asks the Jewish people to proclaim *Shabbat* "a delight" (*oneg*), which will in turn cause them to delight in God.

But what is *oneg Shabbat*? We should enjoy the physical pleasures that God created, so we eat delicious food, wear our best clothes to honour *Shabbat* and enjoy it to the full. But *oneg* should have a spiritual dimension too…

- **Sing** – Singing can unite us and make us happy in a unique way, helping us get beyond thoughts or words.

- **See friends and family** – As well as fulfilling *mitzvot* such as *hachnasat orechim* (hospitality) and *chesed* (kindness), spending time with lovely people is also enjoyable!

- **Sleep** – *Shabbat* is a day for catching up on our rest. As one of the *zemirot* (*Shabbat* songs) declares: "sleep on *Shabbat* is a pleasure".

- **Learn *Torah*** – Make time on *Shabbat* to learn something new. It can expand the heart and feed the soul.

- **Treat every *Shabbat* like it's the first** – *Shabbat* is not about recreation; rather it's about re-creation. If *Shabbat* marks the Creation, then every *Shabbat* is like the world was created anew – a chance to start all over again.

DISCUSSIONS FOR THE SHABBAT TABLE:

1. What do you enjoy most about *Shabbat*? Why?

2. Is your enjoyment of *Shabbat* physical, spiritual or both? How?

3. What can you do this week to increase your *oneg Shabbat*?

QUOTE OF THE WEEK

When the month of Adar begins, one increases rejoicing.

Babylonian Talmud, Ta'anit 29a

VAYIKRA

In memory of
Loraine Young z"l

וַיִּקְרָא

Vayikra

Parasha Summary

The first *parasha* of the book of *Vayikra* is also called *Vayikra*, named after its first word. It means "He called", which is appropriate as it mostly comprises God's speeches and instructions to Moses. The English/Latin translation is Leviticus, meaning the laws pertaining to the tribe of Levi. The book of *Vayikra* describes matters of holiness, especially relating to humans, time and place.

Our *parasha* details various kinds of sacrifice the Israelites brought to the Tabernacle. These include the burnt offering (*ola*), grain offering (*mincha*), peace offering (*shelamim*), sin offering (*chatat*) and guilt offering (*asham*).

1st SEDRA IN:

וַיִּקְרָא
Vayikra

BY NUMBERS:

111 verses
1,673 words
6,222 letters

HEADLINES:

Descriptions of offerings and public law

JEWISH HISTORY: **The York Massacre**

On 16 March 1190 a wave of antisemitic riots culminated in the massacre of an estimated 150 Jews – the entire York Jewish community – who had taken refuge in the royal castle where Clifford's Tower now stands. Antisemitism was rife throughout Western Europe, inspired by the Christian fervour of the Crusaders, which directed aggression against Jews across England, France and Germany on their way to the Holy Land. Rioting had spread throughout England since prominent Jews had been denied entry to Richard I's coronation ceremony in 1189.

After riots had engulfed Norwich, Stamford and Lincoln, they began in York. The Jews were officially protected by the king as his feudal vassals and sought protection in the castle. The rioters, meanwhile, were encouraged by the local gentry, who saw the riots as an opportunity to wipe out the extensive debts they owed to Jewish money-lenders.

Seeing no way to safety, most of the Jews committed suicide. The alternatives were to renounce their faith and surrender to forced baptism or be killed by the mob. They set fire to the wooden keep and killed themselves.

The daffodils – whose six-pointed shape echoes the Star of David – planted on the Clifford's Tower mound provide an annual memorial of the massacre.

For extra on these articles & more visit www.theus.org.uk/shabbatshalom

QUOTE OF THE WEEK

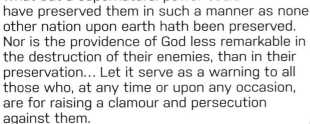

The preservation of the Jews is really one of the most single and illustrious acts of Divine Providence... and what but a supernatural power could have preserved them in such a manner as none other nation upon earth hath been preserved. Nor is the providence of God less remarkable in the destruction of their enemies, than in their preservation... Let it serve as a warning to all those who, at any time or upon any occasion, are for raising a clamour and persecution against them.

**Thomas Newton,
Bishop of Bristol (1704–1782)**

DISCUSSION QUESTIONS

1. Do you think the York massacre is British Jewry's own *Purim* story? How is it similar?

2. Do you think the story of the Jews in medieval England ultimately had a happy ending?

3. Does Jewish history challenge your faith or reinforce it?

PERSONALITY OF THE WEEK
ESTHER

Esther is the greatest hidden heroine of Jewish history, a secret agent who saved the entire Jewish nation, as commemorated on *Purim*. The epitome of grace, beauty and bravery, yet from an unlikely beginning, Esther stood up to the most powerful and corrupt leaders of her generation: King Achashverosh, ruler of 127 provinces, and his Prime Minister Haman, the archetypal antisemite.

A quiet, unassuming woman, Esther was not the obvious choice to be queen, yet she not only risked her life daily by secretly continuing to practise her Judaism, she also showed extreme bravery when approaching the king to overturn his decree to exterminate the Jews. Inspired by Mordechai's words, "And who knows whether it was just for such a time as this that you attained a royal position?" (*Megillat Esther* 4:14), Esther convinced Achashverosh and Haman to attend a banquet and, when she felt the time was right, daringly revealed her Jewish identity, successfully convincing the king that she and her people were worth saving.

Rabbi Akiva, the great *Talmudic* sage, suggests that Esther got her spiritual strength from her ancestor Sarah, the matriarch. Despite everything, she never succumbed to despair and her faith remained intact.

Rebbetzen Eva Chapper

SEDRA:

צַו

Tzav

2nd SEDRA IN:

וַיִּקְרָא
Vayikra

BY NUMBERS:
97 verses
1,353 words
5,096 letters

HEADLINES:
Laws of offerings

Parasha Summary

The *parasha* adds new details about the offerings brought on the *mizbe'ach* (altar) and the work of the *Cohanim* (priests): how the fires were tended, the different types of offerings, and when and how they were made and eaten. One was forbidden to eat an offering in a state of ritual impurity, and if an offering became impure it was to be burned, not eaten. Eating the blood of any animals and certain fats of specific animals was strictly forbidden. We then have the seven-day inauguration of Aaron and his sons, starting on 23 Adar, a week before the construction of the *Mishkan*.

SHABBAT QUIZ:

S   What 'S' should we have three of every *Shabbat*?

H   What do we end *Shabbat* with?

A   What 'A' is the Hebrew word for being called up to the *Torah*?

B   Where in the synagogue is the *Torah* read from?

B   What 'B' is a popular term for Grace After Meals?

A   What 'A' is a prayer we recite 4 times on Shabbat?

T   How many *challot* (loaves of bread) do we have at each *Shabbat* meal?

Answers: S = *Seudot* (meals); H = *Havdala*; A = *Aliya*; B = *Bima*; B = *Benching*; A = *Amida*; T = Two.

ISRAEL GEOGRAPHY
The Etzba HaGalil

The *Etzba HaGalil*, 'Finger of the Galilee', is an elongated area protruding from Israel into Lebanon. There is no geographical reason for this unique shape on the border, but it was included in the British Mandate (and then the State of Israel) because of the heavy Jewish presence there in the 1920s. The Zionist administration prioritised this area, because it contains the River Jordan's four main tributaries. Whoever controls it controls the water in the *Kineret* (Galilee), a vital resource for the population of Israel.

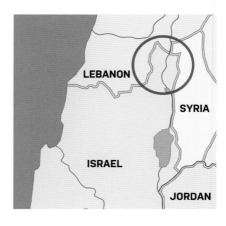

LEBANON

SYRIA

ISRAEL

JORDAN

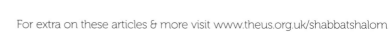

For extra on these articles & more visit www.theus.org.uk/shabbatshalom

PERSONALITY OF THE WEEK
SIVAN RAHAV MEIR

With the rise of social media, Sivan Rahav Meir, an Israeli scholar who is a news presenter on Israel's Channel 2 TV and a popular *Torah* teacher, uses social media and in particular Facebook to teach thousands of students, as well as teaching in person. Her weekly *shiurim* (classes) in Jerusalem and Tel Aviv are attended by hundreds of people.

Born in Herzliya near Tel Aviv, Sivan focuses her *shiurim* on the *Tanach*, especially on the *Torah*. Her compelling teachings bring inspiration, knowledge and contemporary relevance to her students, be they religious or secular. In 2017, some of her writings were published in English as *#Parasha: Weekly Insights from a Leading Israeli Journalist* (*Menora*, an imprint of Koren Publishers).

Like Nechama Leibowitz (see page 61) and thousands of rabbis and teachers, she continues the chain of *Torah* study which originates in *Eretz Yisrael* and then spreads to the Diaspora. This resonates with the prophetic words of Isaiah, which we sing on *Shabbat* mornings before we take the *Sefer Torah* out to be read, *ki mitzion tetze Torah udvar Hashem mirushalayim*- because from Zion shall come forth *Torah* and the word of God from Jerusalem (p. 406 in the green *siddur*).

JEWISH HISTORY
THE ZION MULE CORPS

On 23 March 1915 the Zion Mule Corps was formed. The previous month saw Ze'ev Jabotinsky and Joseph Trumpeldor petitioning the British government to allow them to form a military unit of Jews who were in Egypt having been expelled from *Eretz Yisrael* by the Ottoman Turks. Jabotinsky and Trumpeldor were desperate to help the British to conquer *Eretz Yisrael* from the Turks, in the hope that the British would later support the establishment of a Jewish state there. The British authorities rejected their request, but did allow them to create a volunteer transport mule corps, which played a vital role in the battle for Gallipoli. Led by Trumpeldor and Lieutenant-Colonel John Henry Patterson, 562 Jews courageously supplied the front-line troops. Thirteen men died. This was one of the few Jewish military units since the Bar Kochba revolt in Roman times. It was a precursor to the Jewish Legion, a Jewish battalion in the British Army that fought in Palestine against the Ottomans towards the end of World War One. This contributed directly to Britain's conquest of Palestine, leading to the British Mandate and ultimately the State of Israel.

DISCUSSION QUESTIONS

1. Why was it important for the Jews of *Eretz Yisrael* to fight with the British against the Turks?

2. Do you think the British repaid this Jewish contribution to their war effort?

3. Is it important to have a Jewish army protecting Jews today?

THE JEWS THE WORLD OVER LOVE LIBERTY HAVE FOUGHT FOR IT & WILL FIGHT FOR IT.

BRITAIN EXPECTS EVERY SON OF ISRAEL TO DO HIS DUTY

ENLIST WITH THE INFANTRY REINFORCEMENTS FOR OVERSEAS
Under the Command of
Capt. FREEDMAN
Headquarters-
786 ST. LAWRENCE BOULEVARD. MONTREAL.

Parasha Summary

The *parasha* begins at the climax of the inauguration of the *Mishkan* (Tabernacle). Aaron brings offerings as God commanded. He and Moshe then bless the people that God's presence will rest upon them. A fire comes from heaven, consuming the offerings, and the people fall to the ground in praise to God. But then Nadav and Avihu, two of Aaron's sons, bring an offering that they had not been commanded to do leading to tragedy. Another fire descends, killing them instantly. God later teaches Moses and Aaron some of the laws of *kashrut* (eating kosher). Keeping these laws allows a person to become sanctified and holy.

3rd SEDRA IN:

וַיִּקְרָא

Vayikra

BY NUMBERS:

91 verses
1,238 words
4,670 letters

HEADLINES:

Inauguration of the Mishkan; laws of Kashrut

DVAR TORAH
Keeping kosher

This *parasha* includes the laws of *kashrut*. In a nutshell, kosher animals are those which chew the cud and have cloven hooves, and fish must have fins and scales. There is a list of non-kosher fowl, and insects are forbidden. However, keeping kosher today is not so much checking hooves and scales, but rather checking the KLBD Facebook group for the latest information, and downloading the IsItKosher app to access the 8000-strong product list in a split second (even when offline!).

You would be amazed what food is made of! Common ingredients such as gelatine, glycerine and stearate can be of animal origin, whilst the natural red colour of cochineal (E120) is made from beetles! Even if the ingredients suggest a particular product is fine, 'release agents' (fats used on the production line) might be non-kosher. In fact, even products claiming to be vegetarian can be non-kosher if the factory making them uses the same equipment for products containing ingredients of animal origin.

Fascinating facts about KLBD: (London Beth Din Kashrut Division)

- The KLBD certifies almost 2000 factories in 70 countries across six continents

- KLBD rabbinic inspectors check factories in countries as diverse as China, Malaysia, Egypt, Mongolia, Tanzania, Moldova and Iceland!

- The IsItKosher app gets over 10,000 hits a week

- KLBD licenses over 40 caterers and 30 restaurants and cafes

- KLBD provides free supervision for functions up to 175 people in US synagogue halls

- The KLBD Facebook group has over 8300 members and answers *kashrut* queries virtually round the clock

THE PARASHA IN EMOJIS
one from each aliya (call-up)

1

2

3

4

5

6

7

Answers:

1. *Vayikra* 9:1: On the eighth day Moses called Aaron and his sons and the elders of Israel.

2. *Vayikra* 9:23: Moses and Aaron then went inside the Tent of Meeting. When they came out, they blessed the people and the Presence of the Lord appeared to all the people.

3. *Vayikra* 10:9: Drink no wine or other alcohol, you or your sons, when you enter the Tent of Meeting that you may not die. This is a law for all time throughout the ages.

4. *Vayikra* 10:12: Moses spoke to Aaron and to his remaining sons, Elazar and Itamar: Take the meal offering that is left over from the Lord's offerings by fire and eat it unleavened beside the altar, for it is most holy.

5. *Vayikra* 10:16: Then Moses inquired about the goat of sin offering, and it had already been burned! He was angry with Elazar and Itamar, Aaron's remaining sons, and said...

6. *Vayikra* 11:2: Speak to the Children of Israel as follows: These are the creatures that you may eat from among all the land animal.

7. *Vayikra* 11:45: For I the Lord am He who brought you up from the land of Egypt to be your God; you shall be holy, for I am holy.

DISCUSSION QUESTIONS

1. Do you find keeping kosher difficult?

2. Why do you think some Jews who do not keep some other *mitzvot* are still careful to keep some level of *kashrut*?

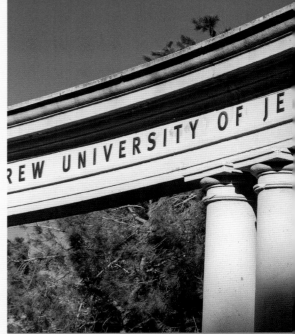

ISRAEL GEOGRAPHY
Mount Scopus

Mount Scopus, or Har HaTzofim, means the 'Mount of the Watchmen' or the 'Lookout Mount' because it gives the best views of Jerusalem. During the Roman period when Jews were unable to enter Jerusalem, it was said that they would come to Mount Scopus to look longingly on the city. Now northeast Jerusalem, it is the original home of The Hebrew University and Hadassah Hospital.

During the War of Independence in 1948, the Old City and East Jerusalem fell to the Jordanians. Mount Scopus remained in Israeli hands but it was surrounded by Arab territory, making the university and hospital inaccessible and unsafe. Both institutions relocated to West Jerusalem. Mount Scopus was designated a United Nations-protected demilitarised Israeli enclave, with fortnightly convoys carrying supplies and personnel allowed in.

During the Six Day War in 1967, Israel gained East Jerusalem. The university and hospital returned to Har HaTzofim (retaining their second campuses in Givat Ram and Ein Karem respectively) and are important institutions in Jerusalem today.

Parasha Summary

God instructs Moses about the laws following childbirth and the *mitzva* (commandment) of *brit mila* (circumcision). The *parasha* then discusses the basic laws of *tzaraat* (similar to leprosy), its diagnosis by a *cohen* (priest), the possibility of a quarantine and the laws of *tzaraat* as it relates to healthy and infected skin. It also considers the status of clothes that have come into contact with *tzaraat*.

4th SEDRA IN:

וַיִּקְרָא
Vayikra

BY NUMBERS:
67 verses
1,010 words
3,667 letters

HEADLINES:
Laws of "tzaraat" and spiritual malady

JEWISH HISTORY
THE SPANISH EXPULSION

On 8th April 1492, King Ferdinand and Queen Isabella expelled all Jews from Spain who refused to convert to Christianity. This 'Alhambra Decree' followed the start of the Spanish Inquisition in 1478, a movement designed to identify (often after torture) Jews who had ostensibly converted to Christianity but secretly maintained Jewish practices. The expulsion aimed to prevent Jews from influencing those who had converted.

On 30 July 1492, 200,000 Jews were expelled and tens of thousands died trying to reach safety. Some Spanish ship captains charged Jewish passengers exorbitant sums, then dumped them in the ocean. Elsewhere, rumours spread that the fleeing refugees had swallowed gold and diamonds, and many Jews were knifed to death by brigands hoping to find treasures in their stomachs.

The Jews fled to various countries throughout Europe and the Arab world, and became known as Sephardim (*Sepharad* being the Hebrew word for Spain).

Afterwards, the Sephardim imposed an informal ban forbidding Jews from ever living in Spain again. They considered the expulsion a terrible betrayal, especially as their earlier times there had been so happy.

The decree was only officially overturned in 1968. Then in 2015, Spain passed a law recognising the descendants of expelled Jews as Spanish citizens, bringing closure to this traumatic event in Jewish history.

For extra on these articles & more visit www.theus.org.uk/shabbatshalom

QUOTE OF THE WEEK

The central aim of text study is to learn how to read a text; that is, that the text must induce the student to think, to make comparisons with the associations that occur to him, to ask and question. The point is that it is not the teacher but rather the text itself that... should bring the student to pose questions and to seek the answers.

Professor Nechama Leibowitz, 1960

PERSONALITY OF THE WEEK
PROFESSOR NECHAMA LEIBOWITZ

The world-renowned Bible scholar Nechama Leibowitz was born in 1905 in Riga, Latvia. She grew up in a home filled with Jewish and general culture. In 1919 the family moved to Berlin, where she taught, wrote and studied. She married her uncle, who was many years her senior, and on the day she finished her doctorate they fulfilled their dream and moved to Israel.

Leibowitz's combination of personality traits – a keen mind, warmth, humour, dramatic flair and insight – as well as her breadth of knowledge made her an outstanding teacher. She began training other teachers while still in her twenties, eventually publishing several works of pedagogical insights into Bible teaching. She received a professorship at Tel Aviv University in 1968 and was awarded several prizes, including the prestigious Israel Prize in the Field of Education in 1956.

She died in Jerusalem on 12th April 1997, aged 92. In accordance with her request, her gravestone reads only 'Nechama Leibowitz: Teacher'. To this day, she still 'teaches' *Torah* to new generations through her books, methods and students, many of whom are prominent teachers throughout the world.

QUIZ ON THE MONTHS

1. In which Jewish month is *Pesach*?
2. Which month has the most *chagim* (festivals)?
3. Which is the month without any *chagim*?
4. Which is the saddest month?
5. Which is the happiest month?
6. During which month do we think the most about our actions?
7. Which months contain half a *chag*?
8. Which months have the other half?
9. Which month has the last letters of both the *alef-bet* and the alphabet?
10. Which month is 'nature month'?

Answers:
1. Nisan
2. Tishrei
3. Cheshvan
4. Av
5. Adar (or in a leap year, Adar II)
6. Elul
7. Kislev/Tevet
8. Kislev/Tevet
9. Tamuz
10. Shevat

5th SEDRA IN:

וַיִּקְרָא
Vayikra

BY NUMBERS:

90 verses
1,274 words
4,697 letters

HEADLINES:

Process of purification from "tzaraat"

Parasha Summary

Metzora continues describing the process of purification for the phenomenon known as *tzaraat*, which causes skin disease in humans and discoloration in clothes and walls. God also teaches Moses and Aaron laws relating to the physical body.

ISRAEL GEOGRAPHY:
The Jordan River

On 10 Nisan, Joshua led the Israelites across the Jordan River and constructed 12 monuments at Gilgal.

The Jordan River runs for 156 miles from north of the *Kineret* (Galiliee) until the Dead Sea in the Judean Desert. It has several tributaries, mostly to the north, including the Iyyon, Chatzbani, Dan and Banias streams. Its name is probably linked to the Hebrew root y-r-d (descent), as the river descends dramatically to the Dead Sea.

Together with the *Kineret*, the Jordan is one of Israel's most important natural water source, second only to Israel's extensive desalination programme. The Kingdom of Jordan also receives 50,000,000 m³ of water from the river, regulated by the 1994 peace treaty with Israel. The *Torah* describes its plains as fertile like "the Garden of the Lord" (*Bereishit* 13:10).

The Jordan features in several places in the *Tanach* (Bible) and is the site of miracles, including splitting to allow the Israelites to cross into Israel (*Joshua* 3:15–17) and the miracles performed by the prophets Elijah and Elisha.

For extra on these articles & more visit www.theus.org.uk/shabbatshalom

JEWISH HISTORY
THE WARSAW GHETTO

As the largest Jewish ghetto during World War Two, the Warsaw Ghetto imprisoned 400,000 Jews within just 1.3 square miles. Despite holding about 30% of the population of Warsaw, it was only 2.4% of the city's size.

The ghetto, established on 16 October 1940, was spilt into two areas: the 'small ghetto', generally inhabited by richer Jews, and the 'large ghetto', where conditions were even worse.

The Nazis closed the ghetto from the outside world on 16 November 1940. During the next 18 months, thousands of Polish Jews and some Romanians were brought in, but the horrendous conditions kept the population at about the same number. Average food rations in 1941 for Jews were just 186 calories a day, compared to 1669 calories for other Poles and 2614 calories for Germans. Hundreds of very young Jewish children went across to the 'Aryan side' several times a day to smuggle food in – often the only source of subsistence.

Over 100,000 inhabitants died due to rampant disease and starvation, as well as random killings, even before the Nazi deportations to the Treblinka extermination camp. Between *Tisha B'Av* (23 July) and *Yom Kippur* (21 September) of 1942, about 254,000 people were deported. It soon became clear that Treblinka meant certain death, which led to the Warsaw Ghetto Uprising in 1943.

QUOTE OF THE WEEK

The most difficult struggle of all is the one within ourselves. Let us not get accustomed and adjusted to these conditions. The one who adjusts ceases to discriminate between good and evil. He becomes a slave in body and soul. Whatever may happen to you, remember always: Don't adjust! Revolt against the reality!

The last letter from Mordechai Anielewicz, leader of the Warsaw Ghetto Uprising, on 23 April 1943

SHABBAT QUIZ: SHABBAT ZEMIROT (SONGS)

1. Which prayer, a love poem, opens our Friday night prayers and is sung at *Seuda Shlishit* (the third meal) as *Shabbat* ends.
2. Which song refers to *Shabbat* as a bride?
3. Which song is based on the *Talmudic* teaching that two angels accompany us home from synagogue on Friday night and bless the family when they see the home prepared for *Shabbat*?
4. Which *zemer* (*Shabbat* song) mentions both the spirituality of *Shabbat* and its physical delights such as rest, *challot* (bread), wine and good food?
5. Which two songs in our *Shabbat* morning liturgy are mystical poems, written in an *alef-bet* acrostic?
6. Which *zemer* uses an animal's rest as imagery for our own *Shabbat* rest?
7. Which *zemer* is possibly the oldest, yet ironically is sung to numerous modern tunes (including a Bee Gees tune and The Muppets!)?

Answers:
1. *Yedid Nefesh*
2. *Lecha Dodi*
3. *Shalom Aleichem*
4. *Menucha VeSimcha*
5. *El Adon* and *Anim Zemirot*
6. *Yom Shabbaton*
7. *Dror Yikra*

Parasha Summary

God instructs Moses and Aaron after the death of Aaron's two sons, who were killed for inappropriately coming too close to the presence of God. God tells them about the priestly service on *Yom Kippur*, during which the *Cohen Gadol* (High Priest) casts lots on two identical goats. One goat is offered as a sacrifice, while the other is sent into the wilderness to die – the 'scapegoat'. Our *parasha* also outlines the prohibition against eating blood and the laws of forbidden relations, both aspects of the life of holiness which God commands to the Jewish people.

PERSONALITY OF THE WEEK
CHAIM WEIZMANN

Chaim Weizmann, the first President of the State of Israel, was born in Russia on 27 November 1874. He studied biochemistry in Switzerland and Germany. While in Geneva, he became active in the Zionist movement, and in 1905 he moved to England and was elected to the General Zionist Council.

Weizmann's scientific assistance to the Allied forces in World War One (especially his invention of an acetone production method, used to manufacture smokeless gunpowder) brought him into close contact with British leaders. This enabled him to play a key role in the issuing of the Balfour Declaration on 2 November 1917, in which Britain committed itself to the establishment of a Jewish homeland in Palestine.

In 1918, Weizmann was appointed head of the Zionist Commission and the British government sent him to Palestine to advise on the country's future development. There, he laid the foundation stone of the Hebrew University, became President of the World Zionist Organization in 1920, and headed the Jewish Agency on its establishment in 1929.

In the 1930s, Weizmann laid the foundations of the Daniel Sieff Research Institute in Rechovot – later to become the Weizmann Institute, a driving force behind Israel's scientific research. In 1937, he moved to Rechovot.

During World War Two, Weizmann and his wife Vera tragically lost one son, Michael, a pilot in the Royal Air Force, in a flight over the Bay of Biscay in February 1942. Their other son served as an anti-aircraft gunner.

With the declaration of the State of Israel, Weizmann became its first President, a role he held until his death on 9 November 1952.

6th SEDRA IN:

וַיִּקְרָא
Vayikra

BY NUMBERS:
80 verses
1,170 words
4,294 letters

HEADLINES:
Laws of Yom Kippur and relationships

ISRAEL QUIZ

1. In 1964 which Israeli snack was created (recently proven to explain Israel's low incidence of peanut allergies!)?

2. In 1977 which Israeli team won the European Basketball Championship for the first time? (They have since won it six times!)

3. In 1984, 7,000 Jews from which country were rescued and brought to Israel in a covert mission called Operation Moses? (Operation Solomon brought a further 14,000 people in 1991.)

4. In 1994 Israel signed a peace treaty with which neighbour, ending a 46-year state of war?

5. In 2008 which navigation app, currently with 100 million users, was invented by Israeli programmers?

Answers:
1. Bamba
2. Maccabi Tel Aviv
3. Ethiopia
4. Jordan
5. Waze

ISRAEL MIRACLE

David Ben-Gurion, Israel's first Prime Minister, once said that to be a realistic person in Israel, you have to believe in miracles! And this little country has produced miracle after miracle in its short history.

In 1948 Israel's tiny, ill-equipped and under-trained army managed to fend off five Arab armies bent on its destruction. Other wars, which sadly followed, had their own miraculous salvations. In 1949 this new country of just 600,000 people took in over a million Jewish refugees from around the world.

Two-thirds of Israel is desert. Yet thousands of people settled there and made it bloom, growing crops and vegetation using ingenious computerised irrigation systems. Israel became one of the world's most educated populations and fastest-growing economies, inventing many of the products we take for granted, such as new computer chips, the technology behind mobile phones and the cherry tomato! And all of this while continuously having to fight for its very existence. Israel is truly a place of modern miracles.

QUOTE OF THE WEEK

Once, in discussion with Lord Balfour, Weizmann asked "If you were offered Paris instead of London, would you take it?"

Balfour looked surprised: "But London is our own!"

Weizmann said, "Jerusalem was our own when London was a marsh."

Parasha Summary

Kedoshim contains many *mitzvot* (commandments). These include not placing a stumbling block in front of a blind person, and leaving certain produce for paupers to take free of charge when harvesting one's field or vineyard. It is forbidden to harbour hatred or to seek revenge, and there is the famous injunction to "love your fellow as yourself", wanting as good for them as you want for yourself. There is a *mitzva* to stand up in the presence of a *Torah* scholar and an elderly person. A judge is not allowed to favour any litigant, and one must have accurate scales, weights and measures. It also contains laws about relationships.

7th SEDRA IN:

וַיִּקְרָא

Vayikra

BY NUMBERS:

64 verses
868 words
3,229 letters

HEADLINES:

Holiness and interpersonal laws

QUOTE OF THE WEEK

The test of faith is whether I can make space for difference. Can I recognise God's image in someone who is not in my image, whose language, faith, ideals are different from mine? If I cannot, then I have made God in my image instead of allowing Him to remake me in His.

Rabbi Jonathan Sacks, 2003

TEL AVIV QUIZ

1. What is the name of the largest park in Tel Aviv (named after the river that runs through it)?
2. What is the oldest neighbourhood, in the south of the city?
3. What is the name of the large non-residential area that houses Israel's Ministry of Defence?
4. What is the name of the main market?
5. What ancient city is also part of Tel Aviv, and forms part of its official name?
6. What is the name of Israel's largest university, in the north of Tel Aviv?
7. What is the name of Israel's national theatre?
8. City Hall is in which square (named after a Prime Minister)?
9. What is the home of the city's three football teams (Maccabi Tel Aviv, Hapoel Tel Aviv and Bnei Yehuda)?
10. Which area, regenerated in 2008 with a different function, is a popular area for visitors?

Answers:
1. HaYarkon
2. Neve Tzedek
3. The Kirya
4. Carmel
5. Jaffa (as in Tel Aviv-Yafo)
6. Tel Aviv University
7. HaBima
8. Rabin Square
9. Bloomfield Stadium
10. Tel Aviv Port

For extra on these articles & more visit www.theus.org.uk/shabbatshalom

A STORY FOR SHABBAT

In 1966 an 11-year-old African American boy moved with his family to a white neighbourhood in Washington. Sitting with his brothers and sisters on their front step, he waited to see how they would be greeted. They were not. Passers-by turned to look at them but no one gave them a smile or even a glance of recognition. 'I knew we were not welcome here. I knew we would not be liked here,' he thought.

Just then, a white woman passed by on the other side of the road. She turned to the children and with a broad smile said, 'Welcome!' Disappearing into her house, she emerged minutes later with a tray laden with drinks and sandwiches, which she brought over, making the children feel at home. That moment – the boy later wrote – changed his life. It suddenly gave him a sense of belonging. It made him realise that an African American family could feel at home in a white area and that there could be 'colour-blind' relationships. The boy, Stephen Carter, is now a law professor at Yale, and in 1998 he wrote a book about what he learned that day, called *Civility*. The woman was Sara Kestenbaum, and he adds that it was no coincidence that she was a religious Jew. "In the Jewish tradition," he notes, "such civility is called *chesed* – the doing of acts of kindness – which is in turn derived from the understanding that human beings are made in the image of God... Civility does indeed require kindnesses toward our fellow citizens, including the ones who are strangers, and even when it is hard."

ISRAEL
TEL AVIV

Tel Aviv was founded as a garden suburb of Jaffa in 1909 and became the first Jewish urban municipality on 11 May 1921. In 1934 it was categorised as a city. Today, Tel Aviv is the most populous city in Israel's coastal plain (Gush Dan), with a population over 400,000 (the only single Israeli city larger is Jerusalem).

The city's name was inspired by Theodore Herzl's play *Altneuland*, meaning 'Old New Land'. A *tel* is an ancient hill with layers of buried civilisation, while *aviv* means 'spring', the season that denotes youthfulness and innovation. The combination of these two words captures the essence of early Zionism and the State of Israel.

Tel Aviv is now Israel's financial and technological centre, and is considered the third largest urban economy in the Middle East, behind Abu Dhabi and Kuwait City. Tel Aviv also has a vibrant cultural scene, and in 2003 its 'White City' (over 4,000 buildings built in the unique Bauhaus architectural style in the 1930s by German Jewish immigrants) was designated a UNESCO World Heritage Site. Many Chasidic Jews settled in Tel Aviv when arriving from Europe, adding to the diversity of the largest modern Jewish city.

Parasha Summary

Parashat Emor deals with three kinds of holiness: holiness in people, time and place. The *parasha* first discusses people: priests (*Cohanim*) and the High Priest (*Cohen Gadol*). As they have contact with the Temple, they must obey certain rules to maintain their sanctity. The *parasha* recaps similar laws relating to ordinary Israelites when they enter the Temple, and defects in animals that bar them from being sacrificed. Then holy time is discussed; the festivals, including the *Omer* period. This period lasts from the second day of *Pesach* until *Shavuot*.

8th SEDRA IN:

וַיִּקְרָא

Vayikra

BY NUMBERS:

124 verses
1,614 words
6,106 letters

HEADLINES:
Laws of Cohanim, sanctifying God's Name and Yom Tov

PARASHA QUIZ (ONE QUESTION PER ALIYA)

1. A *cohen* can become 'impure' for which family members when they die?
2. If a *cohen* becomes 'impure', what two things must happen to become pure again?
3. What must not happen to two generations of animal on the same day?
4. Which is the first holy time mentioned in the *parasha*?
5. Which festivals occur in the seventh month?
6. According to the *parasha*, why do we have to dwell in *sukkot* (booths) on *Sukkot*?
7. Which *mitzvot* from the Tabernacle/Temple are mentioned?

Answers:
1. Parents, wife, children, and siblings.
2. *Mikva* (ritual immersion) and sunset.
3. Must not be slaughtered.
4. *Shabbat.*
5. *Rosh Hashana, Yom Kippur* and *Sukkot.*
6. "In order that future generations may know that I (God) made the Israelite people live in booths when I brought them out of the land of Egypt."
7. The *menora* and the showbread.

ISRAEL
LAG BA-OMER ON HAR MERON

Lag Ba-Omer is a minor festival that falls on 18 Iyar, the 33rd day of the *Omer* (which is what *Lag Ba-Omer* means). It is a day of celebration for two main reasons. First, it marks the cessation of a plague that killed 24,000 of the *Talmudic* Rabbi Akiva's students. Second, it is the anniversary of Rabbi Shimon bar Yochai's death which, according to the *Zohar* (a mystical work), is understood to be the date on which he revealed the deepest secrets of the *Kabbala* (Jewish mysticism). The two reasons are connected as Rabbi Shimon bar Yochai was one of Rabbi Akiva's five surviving students.

Thus the seven-week *Omer* period is traditionally one of semi-mourning, but all mourning is postponed on *Lag Ba-Omer.*

The day is celebrated with weddings, parties, haircuts and hikes. In Israel, the most popular way to celebrate *Lag Ba-Omer* is with bonfires, for which children collect wood for weeks beforehand. No one is certain where this custom originated, but some believe that bonfires signify the light of the *Torah* that Rabbi Shimon bar Yochai brought into the world when he revealed the secrets of *Kabbala.*

The focus of celebrations is on Har Meron, near Tzfat, in northern Israel, Rabbi Shimon bar Yochai's burial place. Every year thousands of people, especially chassidim, camp there. The dancing and singing can be heard for miles around.

For extra on these articles & more visit www.theus.org.uk/shabbatshalom

Jews in Jerusalem demonstrating against the White Paper in 1939

JEWISH HISTORY

On 23 May 1939 the British Government issued the White Paper on Palestine of 1939. This statement of policy was in response to the 1936–1939 Arab Revolt and represented an about-turn in policy towards Zionism and Jewish statehood. The Zionist leadership felt it contradicted both the 1917 Balfour Declaration and the 1936 Peel Commission. Some thought it could even halt the fulfilment of the Zionist dream of a Jewish state.

The document stated that Palestine would be neither a Jewish nor Arab country, but an independent state to be established within ten years. Jewish immigration to Palestine was limited to 75,000 for the first five years (vastly less than necessary to absorb Jewish refugees on the eve of World War Two) and subject to the country's "economic absorptive capacity", and would later be contingent on Arab consent. Stringent restrictions were also imposed on land acquisition by Jews.

The Jewish Agency for Palestine issued a scathing response, accusing the British Government of denying the Jewish people their rights in the "darkest hour of Jewish history" and vowed to fight it until the end.

Parasha Summary

Behar teaches the laws of *shemitta* (the sabbatical year), in which we neither plant crops nor improve the land, which instead lies fallow. God promises us blessings for observing *shemitta* properly. There are also instructions forbidding us to take advantage of others, especially those in a weaker position than us. *Behar* then teaches property and other valuation laws.

PERSONALITY OF THE WEEK
LADY AMÉLIE JAKOBOVITS

Lady Jakobovits, wife of Chief Rabbi Lord Jakobovits, was a refugee from the Holocaust, first in France and then Switzerland. Born in Ansbach, Germany, in 1928 her family moved to Paris in 1936 when her father became the rabbi of a synagogue in the Rue Cadet. The family escaped to Switzerland in dramatic circumstances, returning to Paris after World War Two. Those experiences added a substantial drive to her sense of mission serving the Jewish people.

She married after the war and served alongside her husband as he filled rabbinic positions in Ireland, New York and as Chief Rabbi of the United Hebrew Congregations of the Commonwealth. She became a popular speaker in her adopted language of English and was one of the most beloved, inspirational figures in the British Jewish community. Affectionately known as the 'First

Lady of British Jewry' and 'Lady J', she was renowned for her prodigious energy and care for others. Many charities and individuals benefitted from her dynamic support and enormous kindness. She was widely mourned after her passing in 2010.

9th SEDRA IN:

וַיִּקְרָא

Vayikra

BY NUMBERS:

57 verses
737 words
2,817 letters

HEADLINES:

The Sabbatical year and preventing poverty

A STORY FOR SHABBAT

Once Choni the Circle Drawer was walking and saw an old man planting a young fruit tree. Choni asked the man how long it would take for the carob tree to produce fruit. 'Seventy years,' the old man answered him. 'Do you really think you will be alive for another 70 years to enjoy the fruit from this tree?' Choni asked the man with wonder. The old man replied, 'Just as I was born into a world with fully grown fruit trees planted by my ancestors, so I plant a tree for my children.'

Babylonian Talmud (Ta'anit 23a)

QUOTE OF THE WEEK

I have to justify myself in some small way for having survived the Holocaust by giving myself to others, to those who have less. Otherwise there would be no reason for me to be alive.

Lady Amélie Jakobovits

DISCUSSION QUESTIONS

1. What is the message of this *Shabbat* story?

2. What is the link to our *parasha*'s *mitzva* of *shemitta*?

3. How do we relate technological advances to our belief in God?

ISRAEL A WATER SUPERPOWER!

The world is facing a growing water crisis – at least half the global population is expected to be living in 'water-stressed areas' by 2025. Israel is over 50% desert and has faced recurring droughts throughout its history, so it is facing this challenge head on using technological and engineering initiatives.

Israel's earliest water innovation was the establishment of the National Water Carrier. Planning began even before 1948 and the infrastructure was completed in 1964. It is the country's largest water project, comprising a series of giant pipes, open canals, tunnels, reservoirs and large pumping stations taking freshwater from the Galilee, Israel's largest freshwater reservoir, along an 81-mile route to the south of the country.

Water is also needed for the crops that supply much of the country's food and export industry. Among Israel's inventions is drip irrigation, a technology that has revolutionised agriculture and is now used across the world. It can save water and nutrients by dripping water slowly into the roots of plants from above or below the soil's surface.

Israel's most famous pioneering water technology is desalination, whereby salt and minerals are extracted from seawater to make it drinkable. The first desalination plant was built in Eilat in the 1960s. Today Israel has 34 small-scale brackish water desalination plants, processing about 17 million cubic metres a year, and five large-scale seawater plants. Now over 60% of its domestic water comes from desalination – an achievement unprecedented in any other country. Israel is a world leader in water treatment solutions and has exported its knowledge and expertise to over 40 countries.

SEDRA:

בְּחֻקֹּתַי
Bechukotai

10th SEDRA IN:

וַיִּקְרָא
Vayikra

BY NUMBERS:

78 verses
1,013 words
3,992 letters

HEADLINES:

Blessings and curses relating to mitzvah observance

Parasha Summary

Our *parasha* contains the *berachot* (blessings) that will come to Israel if they are faithful to God, and the *kelalot* (curses) that they will suffer if they are not. The *berachot* revolve mainly around sustenance and peace. Conversely, if the people are not loyal to God they will encounter suffering, as well as enemies who will drive them out of the Land. The *parasha* closes with laws of valuations.

DISCUSSION QUESTIONS

1. Do you believe in miracles?

2. Have you ever seen a miracle? What made it miraculous?

3. Do miracles have to be supernatural? Do they come from God? Can humans perform miracles? If so, are these also from God in some way?

JEWISH HISTORY
THE SIX DAY WAR

Between 5 and 10 June 1967, Israel fought its briefest war. Contributing factors included multiple terrorist attacks on Israel, Syria's shelling of towns in the Chula Valley and attempts to divert the River Jordan's tributaries. Vast numbers of tanks and infantry built up along the Egyptian-Israeli border. Egypt then demanded that the United Nations' Emergency Force abandon all its territories. Egypt's blockade of the Straits of Tiran on 21 and 22 May was an act of war according to international law.

Early on 5 June, Israel launched a pre-emptive strike on the Egyptian Air Force. Within six days, the entire coalition against Israel was defeated. Israeli forces had conquered the Sinai Peninsula, the Golan Heights, most of the West Bank and East Jerusalem. On 7 June Israel conquered the Old City after 36 hours of combat reaching the Temple Mount and the Western Wall.

The world had expected an Israeli defeat at the hands of superior Arab armies. Instead, it saw an unprecedented Israeli victory that some could only explain in miraculous terms.

DVAR TORAH

Around this time, we celebrate *Yom Yerushalayim* (Jerusalem Day), commemorating the reunification of Jerusalem. No people ever loved a city more. We saw Jerusalem destroyed twice, besieged 23 times, captured and recaptured 44 times, and yet in all those years, wherever Jews lived they never ceased to pray about Jerusalem, face Jerusalem, speak the language of Jerusalem, remember it at every wedding, in every home they build, and at the high points of the Jewish year.

Twenty-six centuries ago, the prophet Jeremiah said that a time would come when we would not thank God for bringing us out of the land of Egypt, but rather for bringing our people together from all the lands of the earth. This second exodus, Jeremiah described, would be even more miraculous than the first. We lived to see this day, when Jews from 103 countries speaking 82 languages came to Israel to build not just their lives but the Jewish homeland. After generations it was Jerusalem that bought Jews together from all over the world as one people, in one voice, singing one song.

So long as Jews remembered Jerusalem, we knew we were still on a journey, one on which the Jewish people has been on ever since the first syllables of recorded time: "*Lech lecha meiartzecha umimoladtecha u'mibeit avicha*" ("Leave your land, your birthplace and your father's house"). Never has a city had such power over a people's imagination.

Never did God love a people more and never were a people more loyal than our ancestors who endured 20 centuries of exile and persecution so that their children or grandchildren or great-grandchildren could come home to Jerusalem, *Ir hakodesh* (the holy city), the home of the Jewish heart.

Rabbi Jonathan Sacks

QUIZ
JERUSALEM NEIGHBOURHOODS

1. Where can you buy fruit and veg by day and fish and chips by night?
2. What is Jerusalem's largest park?
3. In West Jerusalem's third oldest neighbourhood you can get a 'house and a garden' and visit national monuments, Yad VaShem and Har Herzl. What is it called?
4. What is the Jewish neighbourhood in the Old City called?
5. Walk through '100 gates' to an ancient world that is very much alive today. Where are you?

Answers:
1. Machane Yehuda
2. Gan Sacher
3. Bayit VeGan
4. The Jewish Quarter
5. Mea She'arim

BEMIDBAR

**Anonymously dedicated
to all projects and organisations
seeking to bring unity
to the Jewish people**

בְּמִדְבַּר

Bemidbar

1st SEDRA IN:

בְּמִדְבַּר

Bemidbar

BY NUMBERS:

159 verses
1,823 words
7,393 letters

HEADLINES:

Formation of the Jewish camp in the desert

Parasha Summary

Our *parasha* begins with a census, the counting of the people, as the first step in preparing for the final journey to Israel. This census counted men between the ages of 20 and 60 – those eligible to serve in Joshua's army in the upcoming battles to conquer the Land. The *parasha* also details the formation in which the tribes camped and journeyed, including the responsibilities of the Levite family of Kehat to carry the sacred objects from the *Mishkan*, including the Ark, Table, *Menorah* and Altars.

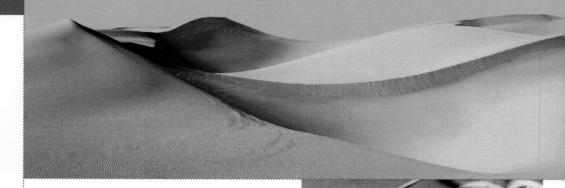

Shavuot in Israel

Celebrating the *chagim* (festivals) in Israel is always very special, as the sense of national holidays being our Jewish festivals always creates an excitement throughout the country. Here are some of the special ways Israelis celebrate *Shavuot*:

* You know *Shavuot* is coming when you pick up your newspaper and recipe booklets drop out. About three weeks before, Israeli newspapers are full of brand-sponsored recipe booklets and pamphlets promising the 'easiest cheesecake' and 'fastest blintzes' to wow your guests.

* In Temple times, *Shavuot* was the day to bring the first fruits of the harvest as well as the first animals born to the flocks, to the Temple in Jerusalem. Today, farmers from across the country take turns bringing fruit and vegetable samples to Jerusalem and presenting them to the President – a highlight in the farming community.

Moshav and *kibbutz* communities also hold elaborate agricultural festivals, often open to the public.

* On the night of *Shavuot* itself, the streets in all the cities and religious settlements are bustling with people of all ages walking from synagogue to synagogue to participate in *Torah* classes. *Tikkun Leil Shavuot* is a centuries' old custom of staying up all night on the night of *Shavuot*, in response to a *Midrash* (Rabbinic teaching) that reports how the Israelites fell asleep the night before *Matan Torah* (the giving of the *Torah*).

For extra on these articles & more visit www.theus.org.uk/shabbatshalom

GIVING OF THE TORAH (MATAN TORAH)

When God gave the *Torah* to the Children of Israel at Mount Sinai, which we celebrate on *Shavuot*, God offered the *Torah* to other people first. For example, God went to Esau's family and asked them: "Will you accept the *Torah*?" They said to God: "Master of the universe, what is written in it?" God replied "You shall not murder" (*Shemot* 20:12). They responded: "But murder is central to who we are and we have always relied only on the sword. We cannot accept the *Torah*..."

... Finally God came to the Children of Israel and offered them the *Torah*. They immediately said: "*Na'aseh venishma* (We will do and we will hear) (*Shemot* 24:7). What is in the *Torah* is of no concern to us. We will commit to the *Torah* and only then find out what is written in it!"

SHAVUOT QUIZ

1. What do we celebrate on *Shavuot*?

2. Which *megilla* (Biblical book) do we read on *Shavuot*? Why?

3. What type of food do we traditionally eat on *Shavuot*?

4. What is the Biblical/agricultural name for *Shavuot*?

5. With what is it customary to decorate the synagogue on *Shavuot*? Why?

6. What special custom do we have for the whole night of *Shavuot*? Why?

7. What special offering did the people bring to Jerusalem on *Shavuot* in Temple times?

Answers:
1. The giving of the *Torah*.
2. Ruth. One reason is that it took place at this time of the year.
3. Dairy.
4. *Chag HaKatzir* (Harvest Festival).
5. Greenery and flowers. Because we learn that Mount Sinai blossomed when the *Torah* was given.
6. To stay up and learn *Torah*. Because the Jews went to sleep the night before the *Torah* was given.
7. The *Bikurim* (first fruits).

Parasha Summary

Parashat Nasso continues to describe the preparations for the Israelites' journey from Sinai to the Holy Land, and contains various related subjects. These include the roles of two of the families from the tribe of Levi, Gershon and Merari; the census of the Levites as a group; rules about the holiness of the camp; the *Sotah*, the *Nazirite* and the Priestly Blessing.

The *parasha* concludes with an account of the offerings brought by the tribes at the dedication of the Tabernacle.

2nd SEDRA IN:

בְּמִדְבַּר
Bemidbar

BY NUMBERS:

176 verses
2,264 words
8,632 letters

HEADLINES:

Laws for Levites and others; offerings from leaders

PERSONALITY OF THE WEEK
PRESIDENT REUVEN RIVLIN

Reuven ('Ruvi') Rivlin, the tenth and current President of Israel, was born on 9 September 1939 into a family which has lived in Israel for generations. A member of the Likud party, he was Minister of Communications and served as Speaker of the Knesset. He was elected President on 10 June 2014.

QUOTE OF THE WEEK

We, as a people who survived the greatest of atrocities and rose from the ashes to be a strong and secure nation, we will do all we can to continue to aid the survivors of the horrors in Syria. We know all too well how dangerous silence can be, and we cannot remain mute.

President Reuven Rivlin, 2017

For extra on these articles & more visit www.theus.org.uk/shabbatshalom

A STORY FOR SHABBAT

The saintly Rebbe of Klausenberg Sanz was famous for his warmth and love. He survived the *Shoah* (Holocaust) but tragically lost his wife and eleven children. On *Erev Yom Kippur* 1947 he was still living in a refugee camp in Germany. As nightfall approached, the Rebbe heard a gentle knock on his door. He opened the door and saw a young girl with tears in her eyes. She explained that every *Erev Yom Kippur* her father would bless her with the Priestly Blessing, but this year there was no one to bless her. "My child, I will be your father this year," he said to her. He placed his hands on her head and recited the ancient blessing with concentration and emotion. The girl left smiling and comforted. A short while later, a group of young girls came to his door, asking for the same from him, and he blessed them with tears in his eyes. As the news spread, the Rebbe spent the rest of *Erev Yom Kippur* blessing all 87 orphaned girls of the refugee camp. None of them ever forgot his warmth and care.

JEWISH HISTORY
THE ANNULMENT OF THE SPANISH EXPULSION

In 1967, Spain passed a law granting Jews and Protestants the right of public worship, including permission to mark their places of worship and advertise their religious services. This was the first such law since King Ferdinand and Queen Isabella proclaimed Catholicism Spain's only religion. It was the first step in encouraging Jews to return to Spain, ending 500 years of exile since the Expulsion of Jews in 1492. The edict was formally and symbolically revoked on 16 December 1968, and in 2014 the Spanish government passed a law allowing dual citizenship to Jewish descendants of those expelled in 1492. Today, around 50,000 Jews live in Spain, mainly in Madrid, Barcelona and Malaga.

DISCUSSION QUESTIONS

1. The Spanish Expulsion was one of the darkest periods in Jewish history. Do you think today's Spanish people feel guilt for this period of history?

2. How do you feel towards countries who in the past participated in Jewish persecution?

3. Can and should they make amends? How could they do this?

QUIZ: SHABBAT BY NUMBERS

1. What 1 do we end *Shabbat* with, while we bring *Shabbat* in with 2?

2. What 2 is found on the *Shabbat* table?

3. What 3 must we have every *Shabbat*?

4. What 4 do we have on *Shabbat*, when we only have 3 on a regular weekday?

5. What 5 does the *Torah* reading on *Shabbat* always come from?

6. What 6 comes before singing *Lecha Dodi* on Friday night?

7. What 7 do we have during the *Shabbat* morning *Torah* reading?

Answers:
1. Candles (1 *Havdala* candle)
2. *Challot* (loaves)
3. *Seudot* (meals)
4. *Tefillot* (services): *Kabbalat Shabbat/Ma'ariv, Shacharit, Musaf, Mincha)*
5. Books of the *Torah*
6. Chapters of *Tehillim* (Psalms) in *Kabbalat Shabbat*
7. *Aliyot* (call-ups) to the *Torah*

SEDRA:

בְּהַעֲלֹתְךָ

Beha'alotecha

3rd SEDRA IN:

בְּמִדְבַּר

Bemidbar

BY NUMBERS:

136 verses
1,840 words
7,055 letters

HEADLINES:

Journeys in the desert

Parasha Summary

Aaron is commanded to light the *Menorah* (candelabrum) in the *Mishkan* (portable Temple). Laws of *Pesach Sheini* are taught, enabling people in Temple times to celebrate *Pesach* if they were unable to do so at the regular time. The Children of Israel receive their travel instructions in the desert. Some of the people complain about their conditions, leading to strife and a plague. Miriam and Aaron speak inappropriately about Moses, perhaps a form of *lashon hara* (evil speech/gossip).

A STORY FOR SHABBAT

There was once a man who loved to gossip. He would often be found around town whispering to his friends. One day, he just couldn't resist telling the rabbi the latest news he had heard. The rabbi ran into his house and brought out a feather pillow. He told the man to rip open the pillow. Puzzled, he did as the rabbi asked. The wind picked up the feathers and blew them all over the village. "Right. Now go and collect all the feathers!" said the rabbi. "But Rabbi, that is impossible! I can't get them all back. They are spread all across the village and beyond!" the man exclaimed. The rabbi looked him in the eye and said, "It is exactly the same with your words of gossip. Once they have crossed your lips, they cannot be controlled or taken back. They are gone forever and spread across the world. Think carefully about that, the next time you are tempted to gossip!"

ISRAEL: **Rechovot**

Rabbi Shmuel Mohilever (1824–1898) was one of the earliest pioneers of religious Zionism. One of his many achievements and contributions to Zionism was to convince Baron Edmund Rothschild to invest in the settlement of Rechovot, thereby ensuring its survival and incredible growth.

   Rechovot is in the centre of Israel, about 12 miles south of Tel Aviv, with a population of approximately 140,000. Its name means 'wide expanses', taken from *Bereishit* (Genesis) 26:22. It was established as a *moshava* (agricultural settlement) in 1890 by pioneers during the First *Aliya*. Today Rechovot is a bustling city with successful industrial areas and its world-famous scientific academic institutions, the Weizmann Institute and the Hebrew University Faculty of Agriculture.

For extra on these articles & more visit www.theus.org.uk/shabbatshalom

QUOTE OF THE WEEK

I shall never forget Shabbat in my town. When I shall have forgotten everything else, my memory will still retain the atmosphere of holiday, of serenity pervading even the poorest houses; the white table cloth, the candles, the meticulously combed little girls, the men on their way to the synagogue. When my town shall fade into the abyss of time, I will continue to remember the light and the warmth it radiated on Shabbat.

Elie Wiesel, Holocuast survivor and author (1928–2016)

QUIZ: GUESS THE CITY IN ISRAEL

1. Daughter of the Sea
2. Roman Emperor
3. Another Roman Emperor
4. House of the Sun
5. Altneuland

6. Information
7. Gateway of Hope
8. Sons of Lightning
9. Head of the Eye
10. Wide Expanses

Answers:
1. Bat Yam
2. Caesarea
3. Tiberius
4. Bet Shemesh
5. Tel Aviv
6. Modi'in
7. Petach Tikva
8. Bnei Brak
9. Rosh Ha'ayin
10. Rechovot

JEWISH HISTORY
Jews return to England

This history of Jews in Britain dates back to the time of William the Conqueror. The first written records of Jews living in Britain are from 1070. However King Edward I expelled the Jewish community from England in 1290. Until the time of Oliver Cromwell the only Jews who remained were those who practised their Judaism secretly but were publicly Christian, mostly Converso Jews, originally from Spain and Portugal.

On 25 June 1656, Rabbi Menashe ben Israel, a leader of the Dutch Jewish community (which mainly consisted of families from Spain and Portugal who had fled there after the expulsion in 1492), petitioned Cromwell to readmit Jews to England. Cromwell wanted to, but he could not convince the government to officially rescind the expulsion, so instead he let it be known that the ban would no longer be enforced. It wasn't until 1753 that the Jewish Naturalisation Act was legislated and received Royal Assent, legally allowing Jews to become full citizens.

Menasheh ben Israel, Rembrandt 1636

DISCUSSION QUESTIONS

1. Can you imagine Britain ever expelling its Jews again?

2. Do you feel fully British and accepted in society?

3. Do you think Britain is a good place to live as a Jew?

4th SEDRA IN:

בְּמִדְבַּר
Bemidbar

BY NUMBERS:

119 verses
1,540 words
5,820 letters

HEADLINES:

Sending spies
to Canaan

Parasha Summary

Twelve spies are sent into Canaan (later the Land of Israel), one from each tribe. Forty days later they return to report on a bountiful land, but ten spies warn that the inhabitants are giants and powerful warriors. Only Caleb and Joshua insist that the land can be conquered, and declare it "very, very good". The people rebel and weep to return to Egypt. God extends their journey to 40 years because of this, and decrees that the entire generation apart from Caleb and Joshua will die in the desert.

The *parasha* also includes the *mitzva* to consecrate *challa* (a portion of dough) to God when making bread, and contains in the third paragraph of the *Shema* the instruction to place *tzitzit* (fringes) on four-cornered garments, so that we remember the *mitzvot* (commandments).

DVAR TORAH
THE LAND OF ISRAEL

Shelach Lecha describes the sin of the spies. God commands Moses to send 12 *anashim* (people) to scout the Land of Israel. These 'people' representing the nation were not ordinary people, but rather the leaders of each tribe.

Ten of the leaders came back with negative reports. Only Caleb and Joshua had a positive approach towards entering Israel. The pessimism caused panic amongst the nation and they refused to proceed. As a result, God punished the nation by not enabling that generation to enter the Land.

However, the *Torah* commands us to follow the majority (*Shemot* 23:2). So why then did Moses not follow the majority's approach? How did the majority of these leaders made such a huge mistake of misinterpreting the reality so negatively?

It appears that the spies viewed the reality of a Jewish state as having potential challenges, which perhaps they were not prepared to accept. Running a state involves dealing with many materialistic issues, which could risk the values and spirituality they had built up. That may be what led them to see the situation in such a negative light. When one has a personal agenda, one's perspective is skewed. That is why Moses chose to listen to Caleb and Joshua, whose opinions were aligned with the will of God and the nation's true interests.

The challenges of running a Jewish State have not disappeared in our times and we should be mindful of this episode.

Rabbi Bentzi Mann

For extra on these articles & more visit www.theus.org.uk/shabbatshalom

QUOTE OF THE WEEK

More than Jews have kept *Shabbat*, *Shabbat* has kept the Jews.

Achad Ha'am (1856–1927)

A SHABBAT STORY

The inspirational Rabbi Paysach Krohn of New York, author of many books including the famous Maggid series of stories (Artscroll/Mesorah publications), is a renowned writer and orator.

Rabbi Krohn has a keen eye for spotting thought-provoking lessons. Here is one example, showing the power of *Shabbat* for both Jews and non-Jews.

The New York Times

In the mid-1990s, *The New York Times* decided to print the *Shabbat* candle lighting times on its front page each Friday. One of its advertising executives even succeeded in obtaining funding from a Jewish philanthropist to cover the cost over a five-year period. Throughout that time, the millions of Jews who looked at that newspaper saw how *The New York Times* promoted *Shabbat*.

The funding ran out in 1999 as the philanthropist scaled back and that seemed to be that.

However, on 1st January 2000, *The New York Times* printed a Millennium edition featuring front pages past and present, from 1st January 1900 and 1st January 2000 respectively as well as projected front page for Friday 1st January 2100. Alongside the news and other items for the 2100 front page was the time for *Shabbat* candle lighting!

The candle lighting time was included by *The New York Times* free of charge. The explanation for this inclusion, by the production manager who was not Jewish, is telling: it is impossible to predict the future for 2100 but it is certain that Jews will light *Shabbat* candles that Friday.

Parasha Summary

Our *parasha* relates the miraculous punishments suffered by Korach and his 250 followers for rebelling against the leadership of Moses and Aaron. The ground opened up and swallowed some of them, whilst others were consumed by fire. Yet the rebellion did not end there. The next day, the people complained that Moses and Aaron had 'caused' the deaths. As a result, a plague killed 14,700 people. God then establishes a way for all the people to see that Aaron was chosen as a leader by causing his staff to blossom, and reiterates Aaron's duties and the need for the *Levi'im* (Levites) to assist him and the other *Cohanim* (priests). Details are given of tithes for *Cohanim*.

5th SEDRA IN:

בְּמִדְבַּר

Bemidbar

BY NUMBERS:

95 verses
1,409 words
5,325 letters

HEADLINES:

Rebellion against Moses

PERSONALITY OF THE WEEK
Sarah Schenirer

Sarah Schenirer, was born into an influential rabbinic family in Krakow, Poland. Her family had ties with both the Belz and Zanz Chasidic dynasties.

She attended a Polish elementary school for eight years. She was intelligent and had a strong desire to learn. She envied the opportunities her brothers had to learn *Torah*.

Recognising her interest in *Torah*, her father provided her with a steady stream of religious texts that he had translated into Yiddish.

During World War I, the family relocated to Vienna, where Schenirer was inspired by a disciple of Rabbi Samson Raphael Hirsch who spoke about the glorious role women had played in Jewish history. Upon her return to Krakow in 1917, Schenirer decided to initiate some educational activity for the women of her community and she began to dream of establishing a school for young girls.

In 1917 Schenirer first set up a kindergarten with 25 pupils, within a few months, the school expanded to 40 students. Word of her success spread and soon other towns approached Schenirer to set up schools. She then started a teacher-training academy to provide the staff for these new schools, which formed the Beis Yaakov movement. The movement grew quickly and soon became the women's educational arm of Agudas Yisrael.

In addition to education, Sarah recognised a need for girls to have female leaders with whom to forge a connection. She was a quiet yet powerful influence, changing the face of Jewish education for women forever.

DISCUSSION QUESTIONS

1. Why do you think Israel places its soldiers in harm's way to rescue and protect Jews who may not be Israeli citizens?

2. As a Jew, how does this make you feel?

For extra on these articles & more visit www.theus.org.uk/shabbatshalom

Man does not live forever. He should put the days of his life to the best possible use. How to do this I can't tell you. I only know that I don't want to reach a certain age, look around me and suddenly discover that I've created nothing. I must feel certain that, not only at the moment of my death shall I be able to account for the time I have lived, I ought to be ready at every moment of my life to confront myself and say – this is what I've done.

Yoni Netanyahu, 1963

JEWISH HISTORY
OPERATION ENTEBBE

Operation Entebbe was one of the most daring rescue missions in history.

On 27 June 1976, an Air France aircraft was hijacked by Palestinian and German terrorists. They landed the plane in Libya, then flew it to Entebbe Airport in Uganda, where all non-Jewish passengers were freed. Despite efforts to develop a dialogue with Ugandan President, Idi Amin, the Israeli government decided a military operation was the best option. On 4 July, the IDF successfully raided the airport and rescued the 98 Jewish and Israeli hostages, bringing them safely back to Israel.

The raid resulted in five Israeli deaths: IDF commander Yonatan (Yoni) Netanyahu, Dora Bloch, who was hospitalised during the raid and was murdered afterwards, Ida Borochovitch, Jean Jacques Maimon and Pasko Cohen.

Though Arab, most African and the Communist Bloc countries condemned the Entebbe Operation, Western countries praised it. The operation greatly improved morale within Israeli society and the IDF. It was an example of Israel's policy to take responsibility for Jews in danger, whether Israeli or not.

The Operation's hero was Yoni Netanyahu (brother of Benjamin, later to be Prime Minister). He had spent much of his youth in America but served in the IDF, joining the elite commando unit, Sayeret Matkal. He was awarded the Medal of Distinguished Service for his conduct in the 1973 Yom Kippur War. Operation Entebbe was later renamed Operation Yonatan in his honour.

QUIZ: ISRAELI LEADERS

1. The first Prime Minister?
2. The first President?
3. The only ever female Prime Minister?
4. The only President to also serve as Prime Minister?
5. The President whose father was the first Chief Rabbi of the State of Israel (and also Chief Rabbi of Ireland!)?

Answers:
1. David Ben Gurion
2. Chaim Weizmann
3. Golda Meir
4. Shimon Peres
5. Chaim Herzog (son of Rabbi Yitzchak HaLevi Herzog)

SEDRA:
חֻקַּת
Chukat

Parasha Summary

Chukat teaches about holiness in the Temple, particularly through the red heifer. Miriam and Aaron pass away. Famously, in this *parasha* the people complain about lack of water towards the end of the 40 years in the desert. God commands Moses to speak to a rock to miraculously bring forth water, but Moses strikes the rock rather than speaking to it. He is punished by not being allowed to lead the people in the Land. Laws relating to the Land of Israel are taught and details of the Children of Israel's battles with their foes are related.

DVAR TORAH

In this week's *parasha*, after the death of Miriam, the water source for the people ceases and they immediately panic and complain. This story explores faith and why it is important.

There was a small town that had not seen rain for many weeks. There was no end in sight of the drought, and the people's reserves were almost empty. The rabbi of the town called all the people together to pray for rain. They came together and cried out with emotion and sincerity to ask God to send the rains they so desperately needed.

A small girl tugged on her father's hand and asked him, "*Abba* (father), if we have all come to pray to God for rain, how come nobody has brought an umbrella?"

UNITED SYNAGOGUE QUIZ

1. Which United Synagogue community is the oldest?
2. How many particpants were there at the first Tribe Summer Camp in 2007?
3. How many participants were there at Tribe Summer Camps in 2018?
4. Which was the first regional synagogue to join The US?
5. Which community has the largest membership as of March 2019?
6. Which has the best *kiddush*?!

Answers:
1. Central Synagogue
2. 14
3. 500
4. Sheffield
5. Borehamwood & Elstree (over 2,400 members)
6. We will leave this to you to debate!

For extra on these articles & more visit www.theus.org.uk/shabbatshalom

PERSONALITY OF THE WEEK
RABBI YISRAEL MEIR LAU

Rabbi Lau is a former Ashkenazi Chief Rabbi of the State of Israel, former Chief Rabbi of Tel Aviv and Chair of the Yad VaShem Institute. He was a child survivor of the Holocaust and his inspiring story represents the rebirth of the Jewish people in Israel after the Holocaust.

Rabbi Lau was born in Poland and was only 5 when the Jews of his small town were liquidated. He escaped with his older brother, Naphtali, but his father, the rabbi of the town, together with his mother and the rest of his family were murdered by the Nazis. Naphtali heroically hid and protected his younger brother (sometimes in a backpack) for three years and through several labour and concentration camps, until they were eventually liberated by American forces from Buchenwald concentration camp.

The brothers remember clearly being instructed by their late father that if they were ever given the choice they should demand to be sent to *Eretz Yisrael*. They sailed to Haifa in 1945 on the boat RMS Mataroa.

Rabbi Lau is the 38th generation of rabbis in his family. Israel's Ashkenazi Chief Rabbi David Lau is one of his sons.

QUOTE OF THE WEEK

From Israel's Declaration of Independence 1948

After being forcibly exiled from their land, the people kept faith with it throughout their Dispersion and never ceased to pray and hope for their return to it and for the restoration in it of their political freedom.

Impelled by this historic and traditional attachment, Jews strove in every successive generation to re-establish themselves in their ancient homeland...

The catastrophe which recently befell the Jewish people – the massacre of millions of Jews in Europe – was another clear demonstration of the urgency of solving the problem of its homelessness by re-establishing in *Eretz Yisrael* the Jewish State, which would open the gates of the homeland wide to every Jew and confer upon the Jewish people the status of a fully privileged member of the comity of nations...

Parasha Summary

King Balak of Moab hears about the Israelite military conquests of other nations. Fearing they will be next, he and the elders of Midian hire the non-Jewish prophet Balaam to curse the Children of Israel. During Balaam's lengthy journey from the east, God miraculously causes Balaam's donkey to speak and rebuke Balaam for his behaviour. Ultimately, instead of curses, God makes only blessings come out of Balaam's mouth.

The *parasha* ends in tragedy. The Israelites bring disaster on themselves by sinning and worshipping Moabite idols, causing a plague that kills 24,000 people – until Pinchas zealously rises up against the wrongdoers.

7th SEDRA IN:

בְּמִדְבַּר

Bemidbar

BY NUMBERS:

104 verses
1,455 words
5,357 letters

HEADLINES:

Balaam's talking donkey

A STORY FOR SHABBAT
RAMBAN AND THE DISPUTATION

Ramban, Rabbi Moses ben Nachman (Nachmanides), was one of the greatest rabbis in Jewish history, whose commentaries on the *Torah*, *Talmud* and other works are still widely studied. When he was nearly 70, he was placed in a deeply dangerous situation. On 20 July 1263 King James I of Aragon summoned him to debate with Pablo Christiani, a Jew who had converted to Christianity and was now a Dominican friar, passionately opposed to Jews being allowed to live in Spain.

Ramban was asked to defend his faith and debate whether Christianity or Judaism was the 'true' religion. The debate took place before a panel of judges, led by the king himself. Though King James wanted a fair debate and allowed Ramban freedom to speak as he wished, Ramban did not want to risk offending the Christians. He debated each point valiantly and wished only for the king to give Jews the freedom to continue to live and practise their faith.

At the end of the disputation, King James I awarded Ramban a huge prize, declaring he had never heard "an unjust cause so nobly defended." On the following *Shabbat*, the king even addressed the congregants of Barcelona's Great Synagogue.

Sadly though, that was not the end of the story. The Dominicans claimed victory and Ramban felt he needed to write his own account of the disputation. The Bishop of Gerona read it and was outraged. He took it to the offices of the Inquisition and the king was forced to try Ramban for blasphemy. Ramban's works were confiscated and burned, and he chose to move to Israel, arriving in 1267.

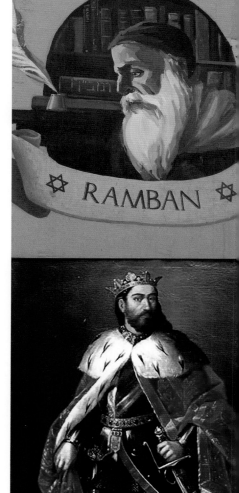

RAMBAN

For extra on these articles & more visit www.theus.org.uk/shabbatshalom

JEWISH HISTORY
EMANCIPATION OF THE JEWS

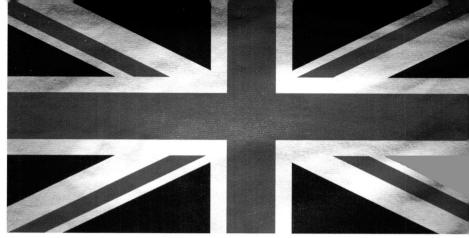

On 22 July 1833 the House of Commons passed a bill for the emancipation of the Jews. This was the culmination of efforts over several hundred years to loosen the legal restrictions set on Jews as a religious minority. Jews had long been recognised as an asset to the UK and this law, promoted by Jews and their allies, sought to win them equality in law.

In 1829 a similar bill had emancipated Roman Catholics, so hopes were high that the Jews could also achieve this too. It took time, but the bill passed on its third reading in the House of Commons by a large majority. However it still needed to be ratified in the House of Lords, where it was rejected in 1833 and 1834. The whole force of the Tory Party and King William IV was against it, but on 31 July 1845 the bill was finally passed.

DISCUSSION QUESTIONS

1. On what basis do you think Jews did not have full legal rights in Britain before this legislation?

2. Are you surprised at when the emancipation of the Jews of Britain took place? (Do you know when the Jews of France and America gained emancipation?)

3. Do you feel you have full legal rights today as a Jew in Britain? Do you face any discrimination?

JEWISH HISTORY
17 TAMMUZ

On 17 Tammuz we fast to commemorate the breach of the walls of Jerusalem, prior to the destruction of the Temple. It also marks the beginning of a three-week period of mourning, leading up to *Tisha B'Av* (9 Av), a date on which both the First and Second Temples were destroyed.

According to the *Mishna* (*Ta'anit* 4:6), other great catastrophes occurred on this date – including Moses breaking the tablets at Mount Sinai following the sin of the Golden Calf, and the Roman general Apostamos burning a *Torah* scroll, setting a horrifying precedent for the burning of Jewish books through the centuries.

Agonising over the events that took place on this day in history is meant to inspire introspection and a commitment to improve ourselves.

Parasha Summary

God praises Pinchas and rewards him with a covenant of peace and everlasting priesthood. We have the next census in the book of *Bemidbar*, this time of the new generation that would enter the Land. During the apportioning of land among the tribes, we meet the five daughters of Tzelofchad. They told Moses that their father died in the wilderness without sons, and were concerned that his name would disappear because inheritance of land went through sons to maintain land within a family. Moses brought their concern before God, who responded that daughters inherit in such a situation. God appoints Joshua as Moses' successor. The final two chapters detail offerings brought daily and at different times of the year, including on *Shabbat* (the *Musaf* offering, which we mention in our *Musaf* prayers) and on *Yom Tov*.

8th SEDRA IN:

בְּמִדְבַּר

Bemidbar

BY NUMBERS:

168 verses
1,887 words
7,853 letters

HEADLINES:

Joshua's appointment as Moses' successor

PERSONALITY OF THE WEEK
RASHI

It is hard to imagine studying the *Torah* or *Talmud* without the foundational commentary of Rashi. Rabbi Shlomo Yitzchaki (1040–1105) was born in Troyes, Northern France. Known by the acronym 'Rashi', he wrote extensive commentary on the *Tanach* (Bible) and much of the *Talmud* and was an authority on *halacha* (Jewish law).

Traditionally, children starting *Torah* study are taught according to Rashi's explanations, which are often printed in a distinctive script.

The main purpose of Rashi's *Torah* commentary is to explain the *pshat* – the simple, straightforward meaning. In doing so, Rashi also quoted those *Midrash*ic teachings that both bring context to the *Torah* and fit into the *pshat* framework. When no

Rabi falomō

single explanation suffices, Rashi quotes two or more explanations, expecting the student to understand how one complements the other.

Being of humble nature, Rashi initially travelled around incognito, leaving explanatory pamphlets in the study halls. Later commentators therefore sometimes called him the '*Kuntres*' (pamphlet).

His work on the *Torah* spawned over 300 analytical commentaries and drew plenty of debate, especially amongst the '*Tosafist*' group of scholars, which included some of Rashi's grandchildren. Even today, every *Talmud* or scholarly edition of the *Torah* contains his commentary or reference to it.

Rabbi Yoinosson Golomb

FROM THE TALMUD

Bruria, wife of Rabbi Meir and daughter of Rabbi Chananya ben Teradyon, was so brilliant and had such a good memory that she learned 300 *halachot* (laws) in one day from 300 sages...

There were some hooligans in Rabbi Meir's neighbourhood who caused him a great deal of anguish. Rabbi Meir prayed to God that they should die. Rabbi Meir's wife, Bruria, said to him: "What is your thinking? On what basis do you pray for the death of these hooligans? One should pray for an end to their transgressions, not for the demise of the transgressors themselves!" Rabbi Meir saw that Bruria was correct and he prayed for God to have mercy on them, and they repented.
Berachot 10a

For extra on these articles & more visit www.theus.org.uk/shabbatshalom

PROFILE
UNIVERSITY JEWISH CHAPLAINCY

University Jewish Chaplaincy supports Jewish students in 12 regions at over 100 UK universities.

Chaplains and chaplaincy couples are there for Jewish students of all backgrounds and affiliations. Together with student leaders, we provide a warm, vibrant and inclusive Jewish environment. From pastoral care to practical support, our goal is to inspire and empower Jewish students – wherever they may be.

Chaplains are also on hand to offer support during challenging times, as students adapt to life away from home, often for the first time. They open their homes for *Shabbat* and holiday meals, offer a listening ear and even give out treats during stressful study weeks. 'DIY *Shabbat*' packs give students the ingredients they need to make *Shabbat* on their own, while chaplain-supported classes and holiday activities enable students to make new friends on campus.

As official members of the university faculty, chaplains advocate for students in a range of situations, including exam clashes and disputes.

The inspiration and enthusiasm that the chaplains provide ultimately helps to shape Jewish lives, Jewish homes and Jewish futures.

We want to help students to uncover their own unique, intimate, Jewish identity on their journey through university, helping them to better understand their place in the web of Jewish history.

Rabbi Mordechai and Lea Taragin-Zeller

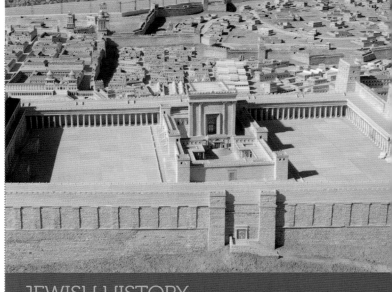

JEWISH HISTORY
SHIVAT TZION

On 1 Av 458 BCE, the Biblical leader Ezra and his followers arrived in Jerusalem. Following the Babylonian Exile and the destruction of the First Temple, Nebuchadnezzer, King of Babylon, exiled the Jews from *Eretz Yisrael* and laid Jerusalem waste. Seventy years later, after Babylon fell to the Persian King Cyrus the Great in 539 BCE, the Jews returned to *Eretz Yisrael*, rebuilt the Temple and restored Jewish sovereignty. Approximately 50,000 returned, a small proportion of the Jewish community in Babylon. Many were reluctant to leave their comfortable new lives and return to *Eretz Yisrael*.

The 110-year period of the return of the exiles is known as *Shivat Tzion*.

DISCUSSION QUESTIONS

1. Do you think you would have returned with the *Shivat Tzion* if you had lived in Babylon then?

2. Can you understand those Jews who chose to remain in Babylon?

3. Do you think you might make *aliya* yourself? Do you think your decision is similar to the decision faced by those Jews in Babylon?

Parasha Summary

Matot begins with Moses instructing the leaders of the tribes about vows and oaths – how they should be kept and how they may be annulled. The Israelites are commanded to wage war against the Midianites because of their hostility. Then there is a description of what is to be done with the spoils of war.

Two tribes, Reuben and Gad, ask permission to settle east of the River Jordan where there is ideal pasture for their cattle. Moses is initially angered, but eventually agrees, on condition that they first join the rest of the people in consolidating the Israelites' position west of the Jordan, as described later in the Book of Joshua.

9th SEDRA IN:

בְּמִדְבַּר

Bemidbar

BY NUMBERS:

112 verses
1,484 words
5,652 letters

HEADLINES:

The battle with Midian and division of the Land

ISRAEL
BAR ILAN UNIVERSITY

On 7 August 1955, Bar Ilan University was founded. Located in Ramat Gan near Tel Aviv, Bar Ilan is Israel's only university with a religious ethos, aiming to "blend tradition with modern technologies and scholarship, and teach the compelling ethics of Jewish heritage to all... to synthesise the ancient and modern, the sacred and the material, the spiritual and the scientific."

It was named after Rabbi Meir Bar-Ilan, a religious Zionist leader who believed there was a need for an institution providing a dual curriculum of high-level *Torah* study with university academic studies.

QUIZ
ISRAEL'S UNIVERSITIES

1. Israel's oldest university (established 1912)
2. Israel's newest university (established 1982)
3. Israel's largest university (29,000 students)
4. Israel's smallest university (2500 students)
5. Israel's only religious university
6. Israel's highest-ranking university according to *The Times Education Supplement*
7. Israel's southernmost university
8. Israel's northernmost university

Answers:
1. Technion (Israel Institute of Technology)
2. Ariel University
3. Tel Aviv University
4. Weizmann Institute of Science
5. Bar Ilan University
6. Hebrew University
7. Ben-Gurion University of the Negev
8. University of Haifa

For extra on these articles & more visit www.theus.org.uk/shabbatshalom

QUOTE OF THE WEEK

There are two ways of knowing. One is called *chochma*, 'wisdom', the other is *Torah*…

Chochma is the truth we discover; *Torah* is the truth we inherit. *Chochma* is the universal heritage of humankind; *Torah* is the specific heritage of Israel… *Chochma* tells us what is; *Torah* tells us what ought to be. *Chochma* is about facts; *Torah* is about commands. *Chochma* yields descriptive, scientific laws; *Torah* yields prescriptive, behavioural laws… *Chochma* has an honourable place within the Jewish worldview. It has religious dignity… *Chochma* is what allows us to understand the world as God's work (science) and the human person as His image (the humanities).

Rabbi Jonathan Sacks, *Future Tense*

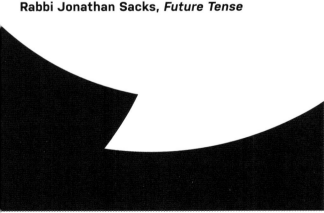

PROFILE: **US CHESED**

US *Chesed*, with the help of over 1000 volunteers across our communities, supports our members and helps the wider community.

Shimon the Righteous, a rabbinic sage from the 4th century BCE, said: "The world stands on three things: *Torah* (Jewish learning), *avoda* (service of God) and *gemilut chasadim* (loving kindness)". This is reflected in the ways in which caring about others is central to the United Synagogue's values. US *Chesed* incorporates US Community Cares, Jewish Visiting, Social Responsibility and *Chesed* Bursary Awards.

US Community Cares aims to ensure that all our members feel that they are part of a community that cares about them. Community Care groups support members throughout their lives with a wide range of services, including befriending, driving members to appointments, regular phone calls, a helpline, walking people to shul, supporting the bereaved, hospital visits, *Shabbat*/festival hospitality or cooking for people in times of need.

We also help our members at times in the Jewish calendar that can be particularly challenging. Each year, volunteers visit those who may be isolated, unwell, recently bereaved or elderly, delivering *Rosh Hashana* cards and honey cakes, and food parcels or vouchers to help people at *Pesach*.

Jewish Visiting aims to ensure that anyone in hospital or prison can have a visit from a Jewish chaplain or visitor if they want. We provide a link between people who would like to be visited and those wishing to do the visiting. US *Chesed* also assists British military chaplaincy.

Social Responsibility encourages participation in projects that make a positive difference to the wider Jewish and non-Jewish community. Together with US volunteers, we run asylum seeker drop-in centres, cook for the homeless, support food banks and engage with domestic abuse charities. We have also organised collections of toys, clothes and toiletries for vulnerable people.

***Chesed* Bursary Awards** enable our young people to participate in Tribe events, regardless of their family's financial circumstances. The US *Chesed* Bursary Fund ensures that the recipients have positive Jewish experiences.

For more information or to volunteer, contact us on 020 8343 6238, chesed@theus.org.uk or www.theus.org.uk/chesed

Parasha Summary

Masei details the 42 stopping points of the Israelites on their 40-year journey through the wilderness, culminating in their encampment on the plains of Moab, where they will stay until Moses dies.

Their destination already close, the *parasha* sets out the boundaries of the Promised Land. It specifies certain places that will become cities of refuge where people guilty of accidental manslaughter are to be protected against possible vengeance from a relative of the person who died.

Masei ends with the leaders of the tribe of Menashe disputing the daughters of Tzelofchad's request to inherit their late father's share in the land. A Divine ruling resolves the conflict: the women have a right to inherit his land, but must marry only within the tribe.

10th SEDRA IN:
בְּמִדְבַּר
Bemidbar

BY NUMBERS:
132 verses
1,461 words
5,773 letters

HEADLINES:
A summary of the journeys in the desert

SHABBAT STORY

Several years after the Temple was destroyed, Rabban Gamliel, Rabbi Eliezer ben Azarya, Rabbi Yehoshua and Rabbi Akiva were going up to Jerusalem. On reaching Mount Scopus, they saw the site of the Temple and tore their garments in mourning.

They saw a fox dart out from where the Holy of Holies had stood. The rabbis began to weep, but Rabbi Akiva laughed. They said: "Akiva, you never cease to amaze us. We are crying – and you laugh?!" But Rabbi Akiva said, "Why are you crying?" The rabbis responded: "Shall we not weep? The place about which *Bemidbar* states: 'And the stranger who draws close shall die' has become a den of foxes! Indeed, this is a fulfilment of the verse, 'For Mount Zion which lies desolate, foxes prowl over it' (*Eicha*)."

Rabbi Akiva answered: "This is exactly why I laugh. Just as we have seen the prophecies of Jerusalem's destruction coming to pass, so too know that the prophecies of her future consolation shall also be fulfilled. I laughed because I remembered the verses (*Zecharia*), 'Old men and old women will once again sit in the streets of Jerusalem… and the city will be filled with boys and girls playing in its streets.' The Holy One, blessed be He, has declared that just as the first prophecies [of destruction] have been fulfilled, so shall the latter. I am joyous that the first have already come true, for the latter shall be fulfilled in the future."

Said the rabbis, "You have comforted us, Akiva. May you be comforted by the footsteps of the Messiah."

Midrash Raba Eicha 5 and ***Talmud Makot 24b***

For extra on these articles & more visit www.theus.org.uk/shabbatshalom

PERSONALITY OF THE WEEK
RABBI YITZCHAK HALEVI HERZOG (1888–1959)

Rabbi Yitzchak HaLevi Herzog was born in Lomza, Poland, and moved to Leeds in 1898, where his father was appointed rabbi. He was already considered a *Talmud*ic prodigy, with a photographic memory and unusual diligence. Secular studies were also of great importance to him. He studied at Leeds University, then followed his parents to Paris and took oriental languages at the Sorbonne. He wrote his PhD at London University on the identity of the '*techelet*' blue dye for *tzitzit*.

He took his first rabbinic position in 1916 in Belfast. In 1917, he was introduced to Sarah Hillman, daughter of the head of the London Beth Din, and they married shortly afterwards. In 1919 he was appointed to the Chief Rabbinate in Dublin. Rabbi Herzog supported Irish nationalist aspirations and was highly regarded by the political and non-Jewish religious leadership of Ireland.

Rabbi Herzog succeeded Rav Kook as Chief Rabbi of *Eretz Yisrael* in 1936. He fought for Jewish immigration and rights in Mandatory Palestine, sought to rescue orphaned children and wrote extensively on how to build a modern, democratic Jewish state compatible with *halacha* (Jewish law). His passing in 1959 occasioned one of the largest funerals ever seen in Jerusalem. His sons, Chaim and Yaacov played prominent roles in Israeli life. Chaim served as Israel's president.

QUIZ
JERUSALEM NEIGHBOURHOODS

1. Which neighbourhood is named after a British man named Moses and is famous for its windmill?
2. Where can you go for a hospital visit, a higher education and the best view of the city?
3. Which *kibbutz* that used to defend Jerusalem's southern approach has now been 'swallowed up' by the growing city?
4. Which 'valley of the giants' was once the main route of pilgrims to reach Jerusalem on festivals, and today is a street with lots of great cafés?
5. What is Jerusalem's largest park?

Answers:
1. Yemin Moshe
2. Mount Scopus
3. Ramat Rachel
4. Emek Refaim
5. Gan Sacher

DEVARIM

Sponsored anonymously in honour of the many passionate volunteers who work tirelessly for our communities

---

Kindly sponsored by Vintage Wealth Management in loving memory of Sandra Stein z"l and Ivor Hartnell z"l

---

Kindly sponsored by Shelley and Merrick Wolman and family

Sponsored by Keith and Lauren Breslauer in honour of Joel C. Breslauer z"l

דְּבָרִים

Devarim

Parasha Summary

The book of *Devarim* takes place during the final weeks of Moses's life, at the end of the 40 years of wandering in the desert prior to the people's entry to the Land of Israel under the leadership of Joshua. Moses begins his series of final speeches, explaining recent Jewish history and the *Torah* to the generation poised to enter the Land. He covers points including the appointment of judges (*Yitro*) and the sin of the spies (*Shelach Lecha*) as well as the recent conquests the people had made against their hostile, threatening neighbours (*Chukat*).

1st SEDRA IN:

דְּבָרִים
Devarim

BY NUMBERS:
105 verses
1,548 words
5,972 letters

HEADLINES:
Beginning of Moses' final speeches to the Jews

JEWISH HISTORY
TISHA B'AV

The saddest day in our calendar is *Tisha B'Av* (9th Av). It marks the destruction of the two Temples and the beginning of the 2000-year exile that continues to this day.

Traditionally we observe *Tisha B'Av* through customs of mourning and sadness, as well as fasting, prayer and introspection. Like *Yom Kippur*, *Tisha B'av* is a 25-hour fast. It is traditionally spent in synagogue reading *Kinot* (liturgical poems and prayers) that lament the loss of the Temple and other tragic events, including the Crusades and the Holocaust.

Tisha B'Av is considered a day of tragedy throughout Jewish history as many terrible events took place on or around this date. As well as the destruction of the First and Second Temples (by Nebuchadnezzar in 586 BCE, and the Romans in 70 CE), it was the day that the 12 spies returned with a bad report from their mission to the Land of Israel; the Romans crushed the Bar Kochba revolt and destroyed Betar (135 CE); Jews were first expelled from England (1290), France (10 Av 1306) and Spain (7th Av 1492). Mass deportations started from the Warsaw Ghetto to Treblinka on *Tisha B'Av* in 1942.

For extra on these articles & more visit www.theus.org.uk/shabbatshalom

DVAR TORAH

Moses, Isaiah and Jeremiah all communicated their prophecies using the word *Eicha*, 'how' or 'alas.' In this *parasha*, Moses speaks to the people about a period of profound frustration. "I cannot carry you alone; how (*Eicha*) can I bear your troubles all by myself?" In the Haftara, Isaiah laments the moral deterioration of Jerusalem and its Jewish inhabitants. "How (*Eicha*) has she become a harlot; a faithful city… in which righteousness would lodge, but now murderers." And Jeremiah describes Jerusalem's destruction on 9 Av: "Alas (*Eicha*), she sits in solitude. The city that was great… has become like a widow."

There is a crucial connection between these events. Moses felt the nation was passive, with people not sharing responsibility for creating a positive society. *Eicha* has the same Hebrew letters as *Ayekah*, 'where are you?' In a sense, Moses was saying 'How can I do this alone, where are you?' This degenerated

further in Isaiah's time. When people of moral stature do not feel a responsibility to challenge hate, a just city becomes a haven for murderers. It culminated in Jerusalem destroying and isolating itself during Jeremiah's era. The three times that *Eicha* is used represent three levels of moral disintegration: passivity, devastation and isolation.

It is currently Tribe's 'camp season'. Summer camp is one of the most powerful Jewish experiences for a young person. In contrast to what *Eicha* represents, camps cultivate the cornerstones of Jewish continuity: community engagement, morality and social responsibility. As we read *Eicha* on 9th Av, reflecting on the negative traits that spanned from Moses to Jeremiah, we see hope in children at camp, building the Jewish people one summer at a time.

Rabbi Eli Levin

A SHABBAT STORY

Napoleon, the 19th century French emperor, was walking in Paris one *Tisha B'Av*. As his entourage passed a small synagogue they heard wailing and crying from within. Puzzled by the commotion, Napoleon sent an aide to see what had happened.

The aide returned and told Napoleon that the Temple of the Jews had been destroyed and they were mourning its loss. Napoleon was indignant: "How can it be I have no knowledge if this event?! Where in the Empire did this occur? Who were the perpetrators?"

The aide responded, "Sir, the Temple was lost in Jerusalem 1700 years ago today."

Napoleon stood in silence and shock. "A people which has mourned the loss of their Temple for this long will certainly survive to see it rebuilt!" he said.

PARASHA QUIZ

1. What happened when the Israelites were about to enter the Land, which meant a further 40-year journey?
2. What was the Israelites' response to the punishment they were given for the spies' sin?
3. Who led the Israelites over the River Jordan into the Land after Moses died?

Answers:
1. The sin of the spies.
2. Remorse, but a resolve by some of the people to enter Israel despite God's warning not to. This ended in tragedy.
3. Joshua.

2nd SEDRA IN:
דְּבָרִים
Devarim

BY NUMBERS:
122 verses
1,878 words
7,343 letters

HEADLINES:
History; The Shema; The Ten Commandments

Parasha Summary

Moses recounts how he prayed very hard to enter the Land, following God's decree otherwise after the sin of hitting the rock (*Chukat*). Moses reviews the Revelation at Mount Sinai and some subsequent sins committed by the people. Looking ahead, he describes conditions of exile from and return to the Land. Details of cities of refuge are provided. The second rendition of the Ten Commandments appears as does the first paragraph of the *Shema*. Moses teaches further laws and gives reassurance to the people.

QUOTE OF THE WEEK

I (Moses) pleaded with the Lord at that time, saying: "O Lord God, You who let Your servant see the first works of Your greatness and Your mighty hand, You whose powerful deeds no power in heaven or on earth can equal! Let me, I pray, cross over and see the good land on the other side of the Jordan, that good hill country, and the Lebanon.

Devarim 3:23–25

DVAR TORAH
The Shema

More than a prayer, the *Shema* is a declaration of Jewish belief. That is why we call it *Keriat* (the reading of) *Shema* instead of *Tefillat* (the prayer of) *Shema*. This first paragraph focuses on our accepting God as the ultimate Ruler in our lives. It contains several *mitzvot*, including *Torah* study, *tefillin* and *mezuza*. We say it in morning and evening prayers and before we go to sleep.

A SHABBAT STORY

It once happened on the battlefield between two warring nations that Jew faced Jew in mortal combat. As one of the Jewish soldiers ran for cover into a foxhole, the other called out, "Surrender, or I'll shoot!". The hiding soldier, quivering in fear, closed his eyes and, crying, recited the familiar words from his childhood: "*Shema Yisrael...*" As the other soldier heard these words, he responded with surprise and emotion, "B*aruch shem kevod malchuto le'olam va'ed.*" As he laid down his gun, he extended a hand to his former enemy and they embraced as brothers.

For extra on these articles & more visit www.theus.org.uk/shabbatshalom

DISCUSSION QUESTIONS

1. The first line of the *Shema*, found in this week's *parasha*, is traditionally the last statement a Jew makes before passing away. Why do you think this is?

2. How does this week's story for *Shabbat* make you feel?

THE FIRST JEW ARRIVES IN NEW AMSTERDAM

Jacob Barsimson was the earliest identified Jewish settler to arrive and settle in the city of New Amsterdam, which later became New York City. He had been sent out by the leaders of the Jewish community in Amsterdam, Holland, to determine the possibility of an extensive Jewish immigration to New Amsterdam. He departed from the Netherlands on 8 July 1654, and arrived on the ship Pear Tree on 22 August. Barsimson was followed by a party of 23 Jews who arrived at New Amsterdam in September from Recife, Brazil (previously a Dutch colony). They established the first Jewish settlement in what would some 120 years later become the United States of America.

JEWISH HISTORY

The Sheriff's Declaration Act of 1835, passed in Parliament on 21 August, allowed Jews in England to hold the ancient and important office of Sheriff – a local government official with various civic duties. The issue that had provoked this legislation was the recent election of David Salomans as Sheriff of the City of London. As a Jew, Salomans was unable to state the final words of the declaration required by the Municipal Corporations Act: "I make this Declaration upon the true Faith of a Christian". The Sheriffs' Declaration Act removed this requirement and Salomans became sheriff. This was another step towards full emancipation of Jews in the United Kingdom.

3rd SEDRA IN:

דְּבָרִים

Devarim

BY NUMBERS:

111 verses
1,747 words
6,865 letters

HEADLINES:

Uniqueness
of the Land of
Israel

Parasha Summary

Eikev is a continuation of Moses' final speeches to the Children of Israel as they prepare to cross the River Jordan and enter the Land of Israel. Moses describes the rewards for keeping the Covenant with God. He warns them of the impending challenges of entering the Land, including the need to conquer the inhabitants there and not be led astray by their religion and culture.

Moses tells the Israelites not to forget that it was God who brought them to this point, and that the success they will achieve in the Land will not be solely from their own hands. If they forget this message they will be exiled from the Land. Moses reminds the people of the journey they have taken under the protection of God. He encourages them to fear and love God and open their hearts to God. Finally, Moses describes the special relationship between the people and God when they are in the Land of Israel, where God

is particularly watching them, rewarding and punishing their behaviour.

The *mitzvot* of *tefillin*, *mezuza* and studying *Torah* are mentioned again, in the verses that constitute the second paragraph of the *Shema*.

PERSONALITY OF THE WEEK
HANNAH SENESH

Hannah Senesh (originally Szenes) was born in Budapest, Hungary. Although her family was assimilated, antisemitic sentiment in Budapest led her to involvement in Zionist activities, and she left Hungary for *Eretz Yisrael* in 1939.

In 1943, Senesh joined the British Army and volunteered to be parachuted into Europe. The purpose of this operation was to help Allied efforts in Europe and establish contact with partisan resistance fighters in an attempt to aid beleaguered Jewish communities.

On 7 June 1944, at the height of the deportation of Hungarian Jews. She was one of 37 Jewish parachutists of Mandate Palestine parachuted by the British Army into Yugoslavia. Their mission

was to assist in the rescue of Hungarian Jews about to be deported to Auschwitz.

She was caught almost immediately by the Hungarian police, and tortured cruelly and repeatedly over the next several months. Despite these conditions, Senesh refused to divulge any information about her mission. At her trial in October 1944, Senesh staunchly defended her activities and she refused to request clemency. Throughout her ordeal she remained steadfast in her courage, and when she was executed by a firing squad on 7 November, she refused the blindfold, staring squarely at her executors and her fate. Senesh was only 23 years old.

She is regarded as a national

heroine in Israel, where her poetry is widely known and the headquarters of the Zionist youth movements Israel Hatzeira, a kibbutz and several streets are named after her.

For extra on these articles & more visit www.theus.org.uk/shabbatshalom

QUOTE OF THE WEEK

Were I to sum up the Basel Congress in a word – which I shall guard against pronouncing publicly – it would be this: At Basel I founded the Jewish State. If I said this out loud today I would be greeted by universal laughter. In five years perhaps, and certainly in 50 years, everyone will perceive it.

Diary of Theodor Herzl, 3 September 1897, following the first Zionist Congress in Basel, Switzerland

SIDDUR QUIZ

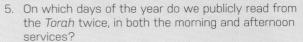

1. How many prayer services are there on a regular weekday?
2. On which days do we add a fourth service called *Musaf* (additional)?
3. What is the name of the fifth service we add on *Yom Kippur*?
4. On what days of the week is there a public reading of the *Torah*?
5. On which days of the year do we publicly read from the *Torah* twice, in both the morning and afternoon services?
6. What does the word *siddur* mean and why is it an appropriate name for a prayer book?
7. What is the central prayer of each service called?
8. What is the name of the special collection of *Tehillim* (Psalms) said in praise on special days such as *Rosh Chodesh*, *Chanukah* and *Yom Tov*?
9. What is the name of the specific liturgy of the United Synagogue and similar communities in the UK?
10. Who was the first person to codify the prayers into the earliest form of the *siddur*?

Answers:
1. Three
2. *Shabbat*, *Rosh Chodesh* (the New Moon), *Yom Tov*, *Rosh HaShana* and *Yom Kippur*
3. *Neila*
4. Monday, Thursday and *Shabbat*
5. *Shabbat* and fast days
6. Order, as it presents all the prayers in an organised, orderly way
7. *Amida* (standing prayer) or *Shemona Esrei* (literally 18, because of the original 18 blessings of the weekday *Amida*)
8. *Hallel*
9. *Minhag Anglia*
10. Rabbi Amram Gaon

Parasha Summary

Many laws relating to the Land are taught, along with blessings for the keeping the laws and curses for not doing so. Permission to eat meat is detailed. Following a false prophet, encouraging people to go astray and pursuing practices not rooted in Judaism are forbidden. Further laws of *kashrut* are taught, along with more details of our responsibilities to other people. The *parasha* ends with additional details relating to *Pesach*, *Shavout* and *Succot*.

4th SEDRA IN:

דְּבָרִים

Devarim

BY NUMBERS:

126 verses
1,932 words
7,442 letters

HEADLINES:

Avoiding things which distance you from God

DVAR TORAH: Elul – seizing the moment!

The *Mishna Berura*, one of the most prominent 20th century works of Jewish law, gives four reasons for the importance of the month of *Elul*:

1) At the start of *Elul*, Moses ascended Mount Sinai to receive the second set of tablets. We sound the shofar from 1 *Elul* to ensure the Jewish people would not return to idolatry and revisit previous mistakes.

2) In the phrase in *The Song of Songs*, "I am for my beloved and my beloved is for me" – אני לדודי ודודי לי, the first letters of each word spell *Elul*. Our 'Beloved' (God) will be for us if we will (first) be for God.

3) The last letter of those four words is י, with the numerical value of ten. Four times ten is 40, the number of days from 1 *Elul* until *Yom Kippur*, again illustrating the precious opportunity of these days for re-engaging with God.

4) *Elul* is also an acronym of a phrase from *Devarim*: 'and the Lord your God will circumcise your heart and the hearts of your offspring to love the Lord your God' - ומל ה' אלוקיך את לבבך ואת לבב זרעך. We should be aware of the great assistance that God extends to sincere penitents – even, according to the book *Sha'arei Teshuva*, when their natural abilities might not be sufficient.

But of what direct import are these themes to us and how are we to practically incorporate them into our own *Elul* preparations?

The *Talmud* (*Rosh Hashana* 16b) teaches that a person is judged on *Rosh Hashana* "according to their thoughts and deeds 'in the moment'..." – not on what we have previously done or may do in future.

The challenge on *Rosh Hashana* is to stand before our Maker, in the 'here and now', as worthy, well focused, committed and highly motivated people. We need to shed the negativity and cynicism of the past and embrace a new, bolder and more positive present and future.

Elul is the time to ensure that we will succeed in this regard. It is our 'reset button', when, through hearing the rallying call of the *Shofar*, re-engaging positively with God and our fellow beings and improving our attitude and behaviour, we will be empowered to 'seize the moment' on *Rosh Hashana*. Having 'reset' ourselves throughout *Elul* we can stand before God with some measure of confidence on *Rosh Hashana*, knowing how much He wants us to succeed – even beyond the limit of our own expectations!

Rabbi Mordechai Ginsbury

For extra on these articles & more visit www.theus.org.uk/shabbatshalom

PERSONALITY OF THE WEEK
CHIEF RABBI EPHRAIM MIRVIS

Chief Rabbi Ephraim Mirvis was born on *Rosh Hashana*, 1956 in Johannesburg, South Africa. He is only the 11th Chief Rabbi since the office was introduced in 1704. He is the religious figurehead for Jewish communities right across the Commonwealth, from Hull to Hong Kong and from Cardiff to Cochin. He was installed on 1 September 2013 in an historic ceremony attended by HRH The Prince of Wales. He has previously served as Chief Rabbi of Ireland and, most recently, as rabbi of Finchley Synagogue (Kinloss) in London and is one of the UK's most respected faith leaders.

As Chief Rabbi, he is a primary representative of the Jewish community to government, other faiths and civil society and is responsible for oversight of crucial parts of the UK Jewish community's religious infrastructure.

Chief Rabbi Mirvis is known as a principled leader who has broken new ground in the fields of interfaith and social responsibility, as well as being a champion of faith communities which strike an essential balance between the particular values which make them unique and the universal human values which we all share.

The Chief Rabbi makes community visits across the UK and the Commonwealth a priority, to provide inspiration and Torah education. He has launched a number of innovative projects, such as the Ma'ayan female educators programme, Neshama, the Ben Azzai social responsibility programme and, of course, ShabbatUK which inspired this book!

Follow the Chief Rabbi on Facebook (@ChiefRabbiMirvis), Twitter (@ ChiefRabbi) or learn more at www.chiefrabbi.org

JEWISH HISTORY
THE OUTBREAK OF WORLD WAR TWO

On 1 September 1939 Germany invaded Poland, killing thousands of Jewish and other civilians. Out of the 3,351,000 Jews in Poland, 2,042,000 came under Nazi rule while 1,309,000 came under Soviet rule (the Soviets invaded Poland from the east). The UK responded with an ultimatum to Germany to cease military operations. This was ignored and on 3 September the UK declared war on Germany.

During the war, 1.5 million Jews fought on the side of Allied forces, including 26,000 from Palestine and 90,000 from the British Commonwealth.

World War Two was the deadliest conflict in human history, with between 50 and 85 million fatalities, mostly civilians. Included in that number were 6 million Jews massacred in the Holocaust, two thirds of European Jewry.

DISCUSSION QUESTIONS

1. Did World War Two change Jewish history forever? How?

2. Is it important to study history? Should we study world history generally or only when it intersects with Jewish history?

Parasha Summary

Moses instructs the people of Israel to appoint judges and law enforcement officers in every city, to pursue justice and meticulously administer it without corruption or favouritism.

Shofetim also includes prohibitions against idolatry and sorcery, laws governing the appointment and behaviour of a king, guidelines for the creation of 'cities of refuge' in the event of manslaughter, and laws of war. We learn the prohibition against wanton destruction of something of value, exemplified by the law that forbids to cut down a fruit tree when laying siege. The *parasha* concludes with the law relating to a criminal case for which no clear evidence of guilt can be ascertained.

5th SEDRA IN:

דְּבָרִים

Devarim

BY NUMBERS:

97 verses
1,523 words
5,590 letters

HEADLINES:

Jewish public and governmental law

DVAR TORAH: The art of sensitivity

And the officers [of war] shall speak further to the people...: "Who is the person that is fearful and faint-hearted? Let him go and return to his house, and let him not make the heart of his brother faint like his heart!" (Devarim 20:8)

Prior to this, the *Torah* describes three other categories of people who are also to be excused from battle: someone who has built a house but not dedicated it; someone who planted a vineyard but has not partaken of its fruits; and someone who is engaged but not married.

Rabbi Yossi HaGalili (*Talmud* Sota 44a) explains that the fourth category refers to someone who fears he is unworthy of being saved because of his transgressions. Rabbi Yossi adds that this is the reason why the other three categories were told to go home. If someone had to leave because of his sins, he would be embarrassed. But since other groups were also sent home, people would not know who was leaving for which reason.

This is amazing! The *Torah* instructs us that large numbers of soldiers were sent home in wartime solely to protect a few people from humiliation and embarrassment.

Often at this time of the year, we should be starting to think about how to prepare for *Rosh Hashana*. Before we can appear before the Judge, God, we are asked to look at how we have behaved with the people around us, and consider the levels of sensitivity and understanding that we show them.

Rabbi Alan Garber

For extra on these articles & more visit www.theus.org.uk/shabbatshalom

London Beth Din
Court of the Chief Rabbi

THE LONDON BETH DIN
(THE CHIEF RABBI'S COURT)

Within 50 years of Jewish resettlement in the UK in 1656, the offices of the Chief Rabbi and the London Beth Din (court of law) were established to provide a central religious authority for communities throughout the UK.

The activities of the London Beth Din include *dinei Torah* (court cases), *gittin* (divorces), *geirut* (conversions), *shechita* (Jewish slaughter), *kashrut* and as well as advice and rulings on matters of Jewish law for individuals and the wider community. The dayanim (judges) of the London Beth Din have advanced rabbinic ordination and also serve as dayanim for the Council of European Rabbis, supporting communities that cannot maintain Beth Din services. The Dayanim provide mentoring support and specialist advice for rabbis, educators and other professionals.

The dayanim are Dayan Menachem Gelley (Rosh Beth Din), Dayan Yonason Abraham, Dayan Ivan Binstock and Dayan Shmuel Simons. Dayan Chanoch Ehrentreu, formerly the head of the Beth Din, now serves in a consultancy role since his retirement from the day-to-day work of the Beth Din.

DISCUSSION QUESTIONS

1. Why is it important to have a Beth Din in the community?

2. How is the Beth Din different from the civil courts in Britain?

Dayan Menachem Gelley

Dayan Yonason Abraham

Dayan Ivan Binstock

Dayan Shmuel Simons

A STORY FOR SHABBAT

When the Romans had forbidden Jews from learning *Torah* in *Eretz Yisrael*, Rabbi Akiva continued to teach *Torah* to his students. "Aren't you scared that the Romans will catch you?" he was once asked. He replied with this story.

A fox was walking along a riverbank and noticed fish darting from place to place in the river. "What are you swimming away from?" he asked them. They replied, "We are fleeing from the nets that humans use to try and catch us." The wily fox asked, "Why don't you come and live with me on dry land then?" The fish replied, "Oh fox! They say the fox is one of the cleverest animals, but you are not clever at all. If we are afraid when we are in the water, a place that gives us life, then how can we live on dry land, a place of death for us?"

Rabbi Akiva said, "So too with us. If we are scared while we learn *Torah*, our life source, then imagine how our lives would be if we stop learning *Torah*?"

JEWISH HISTORY
DAF YOMI

On 11 September 1923 the Daf Yomi programme was initiated by Rabbi Meir Shapiro of Lublin, Poland. Tens of thousands of people across the world study the same page (*daf*) of *Gemara* on the same day (*yom*), completing the whole of the *Talmud* (known as *Shas*) in seven and a half years! We are at the time of writing coming to the end of the thirteenth cycle, with the next *Siyum HaShas* (completion of the *Talmud* cycle) due in January 2020.

כִּי־תֵצֵא
Ki Teitzei

6th SEDRA IN:
דְּבָרִים
Devarim

BY NUMBERS:
110 verses
1,582 words
5,856 letters

HEADLINES:
Many laws, relating to both God and to humans

Parasha Summary

Ki Teitzei has the largest number of *mitzvot* in a single *parasha*, covering many aspects of life. It delineates various civil and criminal laws, including those regarding relationships, loans, vows and divorce. A theme is concern and protection for people in difficult circumstances who are at a disadvantage.

The *parasha* concludes with the *mitzva* of remembering the attacks which *Amalek* made against the Israelites. This section is also read on the *Shabbat* before *Purim, Shabbat Zachor,* as a yearly fulfilment of this remembrance.

PERSONALITY OF THE WEEK
RABBI JOSEPH B. SOLOVEITCHIK (1903-1993)

Rabbi Soloveitchik was born in Pruzhan, Poland, a scion of a famous rabbinic family. He was a remarkable scholar of *Talmud*, Jewish law and philosophy. After intensive *Torah* studies under his father's tutelage, he attended the University of Berlin where he was awarded a PhD in philosophy. He later founded the Maimonides High School in Boston, Massachusetts, having immigrated to the USA in 1932 with his wife Tonya.

In 1941, he succeeded his father (after the latter's passing) as Rosh Yeshiva of the Rabbi Isaac Elchanan Theological Seminary at Yeshiva University in New York, a position he held until his passing in 1993. Hugely influential, he ordained over 2,000 rabbis, inspired thousands of other people and wrote important works of Jewish scholarship and philosophy such as *The Lonely Man of Faith* and *Halakhic Man*. His teachings on the application and relevance of Judaism in modernity remain critically important, inspiring generations which followed him.

For extra on these articles & more visit www.theus.org.uk/shabbatshalom

QUOTE OF THE WEEK

We are proud of our pioneering role in the creation of the State of Israel. We are proud to stand here today together with Prime Minister Netanyahu and declare our support for Israel. And we are proud of the relationship we have built with Israel. And as we mark 100 years since Balfour, we look forward to taking that relationship even further.

Prime Minister Theresa May, November 2017, during the centenary celebrations for the Balfour Declaration

ISRAEL
The Supreme Court

The Supreme Court in Jerusalem, which is the highest court in Israel and the final court of appeal, was inaugurated on 14 September 1948. It consists of 15 Justices and two Registrars. The President of the Supreme Court heads the entire judicial system.

QUIZ: ISRAELI LAW TRUE OR FALSE?

1. Israeli law is based on a mixture of Turkish, British and *Talmudic* law.
2. All matters of personal status (marriages, divorces and conversions) are handled by the civil courts.
3. No non-Jews are represented on the Supreme Court.
4. None of the Supreme Court justices are women.
5. Dorothy de Rothschild, who donated the 1992 Supreme Court Building, was the daughter-in-law of Lord Rothschild, who received the Balfour Declaration.

Answers:
1. True
2. False – they are dealt with by religious courts
3. False – there is currently an Israeli Arab Supreme Court Justice and one has recently retired
4. False – 30% are currently women (compared with 25% in UK), including the President, Chief Justice Esther Hayut
5. False. Dorothy was the daughter-in-law of his cousin, Edmond James de Rothschild, the famous benefactor of the First *Aliya*, from the French branch of the Rothschild family

JEWISH HISTORY
ANNE FRANK

Anne Frank is one of the most discussed victims of the Holocaust, gaining publicity after her death due to the publication of the diaries she kept throughout her teenage years in a volume entitled 'The Diary of a Young Girl'. It has since been translated into over 60 languages and is a best-seller around the world.

Anne was born in Frankfurt in 1929 but moved to Amsterdam when the Nazi Party took control of Germany. Her family lost their citizenship in 1941, becoming stateless. Persecution of the Jews increased further when the Germans invaded the Netherlands, leading to the Frank family hiding in a concealed annex in the building in which Anne's father, Otto, worked in July 1942. Later on, the Frank family were joined by another Jewish family: the Van Pels.

Employees of the firm Otto worked in were the only connection between the family and the outside world, keeping them updated with news of the war and also supplying them with food. These people were aware that if they were caught, they would be punished with the death penalty, making their act of extreme bravery all the more remarkable.

In August 1944 the Jewish families were betrayed. The annex was stormed by German officers and the inhabitants were sent to Westerbork transit camp and were later deported to Auschwitz. Anne and her sister, Margot, were later moved to Bergen-Belsen where they died just a few months before the camps were liberated.

For extra on these articles & more visit www.theus.org.uk/shabbatshalom

Parasha Summary

Moses continues his farewell speech, preparing the Israelites further for their future national life living in their own land, the Land of Israel. This includes agricultural laws such as the first fruits (*bikkurim*), the seven-year agricultural cycle culminating in the sabbatical year (*shemitta*) and a general appeal to keep all the *mitzvot* (commandments) once the Israelites cross the Jordan and settle into their new lives. He then instructs the people to build a monument of stones after crossing the Jordan, with the words of the *Torah* inscribed on them. The *parasha* ends with a description of blessings and curses.

PARASHA QUIZ

1. Where should you take the first fruits?
2. True or false, *Bikkurim* applies only to the seven speices for which the Land of Israel is praised?
3. Who gets to eat the tithes during the third and sixth years of the agricultural cycle?
4. What honourable description does the *Torah* give the Jewish people?
5. What was written on the stones that were set up after crossing the Jordan?
6. Who stood on Mount Gerizim?
7. How many verses describe the blessings and how many describe the curses?
8. Which tribes settled in the lands of Sichon of Cheshbon and Og of Bashan?

Answers:
1. To the *Cohen* (priest) at the Temple in Jerusalem
2. True. They are wheat, barley, grapes, figs, pomegranates, olive and dates
3. The Levite, the stranger, the orphan and the widow
4. *Am Segula* (treasured people)
5. The words of the *Torah*
6. Simeon, Levi, Judah, Issachar, Joseph and Benjamin
7. Eight for the blessings, 55 for the curses
8. Reuben, Gad and parts of Menashe

7th SEDRA IN:

דְּבָרִים

Devarim

BY NUMBERS:

122 verses
1,747 words
6,811 letters

HEADLINES:

Obligation to take first fruits to the Temple; blessings & curses

ISRAEL
OPERATION MAGIC CARPET

On 25 September 1950, the final airlift of Yemenite Jews during Operation Magic Carpet touched down in Israel. The operation began in May 1949, after the authorities in Yemen agreed to let the Jewish community of approximately 50,000 leave. The operation consisted of 380 secret flights of transport planes to Israel. It only became public weeks later, for fear that Arab pressure on the Yemenite government would halt the operation.

JEWISH HISTORY
THE DREYFUS AFFAIR

Le Petit Journal
SUPPLEMENT ILLUSTRÉ

ALFRED DREYFUS DANS SA PRISON

Alfred Dreyfus was a captain in the French army and an assimilated Jew. He was falsely convicted of passing military secrets to France's enemy, Germany, after a French spy at the German Embassy in Paris discovered a ripped-up letter in a waste basket in 1894, with handwriting said to resemble that of Dreyfus. Dreyfus was court-martialled, found guilty of treason and sentenced to life behind bars on Devil's Island off French Guiana. In fact, the real culprit was a French intelligence officer, Major Esterhazy. He was protected by some of his colleagues who preferred to blame Dreyfus since he was a Jew.

In a public ceremony in Paris following his conviction, Dreyfus had the insignia torn from his uniform and his sword broken. He was paraded before a crowd that shouted, "Death to Judas, death to the Jew." This scandal, which revealed systematic antisemitism in French society and institutions, rocked France in the late 19th and early 20th centuries.

Known as the Dreyfus Affair, it had a deep impact on Jewish history. It led Theodor Herzl, who was reporting on the trial for the Viennese newspaper, Neue Freie Presse, to realise that the only solution to the problem of antisemitism and the place of the Jew in European society was to create a Jewish state. Compelling new evidence came to light showing Dreyfus's innocence. Pressure mounted by famous writer Emile Zola led to a retrial, but still Dreyfus was not exonerated, in another shocking act of antisemitism.

Dreyfus was finally pardoned in 1899 by direct order of the President of France, yet only exonerated seven years later.

QUOTE OF THE WEEK

You can't drive away the darkness with sticks or weapons. The only way is to light a candle and the darkness will disappear by itself. Our candle is the *Torah*.

Rabbi Yisrael Meir Kagan, the Chafetz Chaim (1839–1933)

DISCUSSION QUESTIONS

1. The irony of the country where the Dreyfus Affair took place was not lost on Herzl. Why is it ironic that this took place in France (clue: 1789)?

2. Why do you think the Dreyfus Affair led Herzl to the conclusion that creating a state for the Jews was the only solution to antisemitism?

3. Is there still antisemitism in Europe today? Does this mean Herzl was right?

SEDRA:

נִצָּבִים

Nitzavim

Parasha Summary

Moses continues his farewell speech, delivering a rousing sermon designed to inspire the Israelites to strengthen their faith in God. He begins by urging the people to renew the Covenant their ancestors made with God, highlighting the eternal nature of the Covenant which has been made with previous, present, and future generations. Moses then warns the people of the dangerous allure of idol worship.

The *parasha* ends with powerful and inspiring words, the choice presented to all Jews: "I have called heaven and earth today as witnesses against you. I have set life and death before you, blessing and curse. Choose life, so that you and your descendants may live to love your God."

8th SEDRA IN:

דְּבָרִים

Devarim

BY NUMBERS:

30 verses
553 words
2,123 letters

HEADLINES:

Promise of our eventual redemption

THE JEWISH CALENDAR IN ISRAEL

Rosh Hashana signifies the beginning of the Jewish year and Hebrew calendar. The Hebrew calendar is the official calendar of the State of Israel, as legislated by the Knesset on 19 July 2016. The law states:

"The Hebrew calendar is the official calendar of the State and alongside it the Gregorian calendar will be used as an official calendar. Use of the Hebrew calendar and the Gregorian calendar will be determined by law."

For extra on these articles & more visit www.theus.org.uk/shabbatshalom

PERSONALITY OF THE WEEK
CHIEF RABBI LORD JONATHAN SACKS

Rabbi Lord Jonathan Sacks served as Chief Rabbi from 1991 – 2013.

As one of the world's pre-eminent faith leaders and thinkers, Rabbi Sacks has come to personify a Judaism of intellectual integrity, ethical passion and spiritual power. Through his writings and speeches, he has called for a Judaism that engages with the world and is emboldened by such engagement, arguing that there is no contradiction, not even a conflict, between contributing to humanity and affirming our distinctive identity.

This approach has led to Rabbi Sacks being a frequent and sought-after contributor to radio, television and the press both in Britain and around the world. Described by HRH The Prince of Wales as "a light unto this nation", and the recipient of several prestigious awards, including the 2016 Templeton Prize, Rabbi Sacks was knighted by HM Queen Elizabeth II in 2005 and made a Life Peer, taking his seat in the House of Lords in October 2009.

Rabbi Sacks has published over 30 books covering a wide range of fields such as history, faith, politics, philosophy and science, and has written commentaries and translations to the familiar 'green' siddur used in many communities and the Koren Sacks series of Machzorim prayer books for Yom Tov. His weekly 'Covenant & Conversation' essays on the weekly parasha, now also produced as a Family Edition, have a global audience.

A prolific user of social media, Rabbi Sacks' website (www.rabbisacks.org) and Facebook and Twitter profiles (@RabbiSacks) are a tremendous resource for Jewish learning, and include articles, educational material, speeches and videos.

A graduate of Yeshivat Etz Chaim, Cambridge, Oxford and London (King's College) universities, Rabbi Sacks also studied at Jews' College, where he later served as College principal. Before being appointed Chief Rabbi, he was the rabbi of the Golders Green and Marble Arch synagogues. He is married to Lady Elaine Sacks.

A STORY FOR SHABBAT

In Spain in 1497 there were no longer any synagogues, schools or other Jewish institutions. But as many as 300,000 Jews chose to stay and convert, while practising their Judaism in secret. They were called crypto-Jews (secret Jews), conversos or anusim (those forced to abandon their Jewish practice). As Rosh Hashana approached, the anusim dreamed of the days when they could openly fulfil the mitzva of blowing the shofar. But they could no longer do so, as even the quietest of shofar sounds could be discovered by Christian neighbours, who could then inform the Spanish Inquisition, leading to capture, torture and death.

Don Fernando Aguilar was the chief conductor of the Royal Barcelona Orchestra, a master musician – and a converso. On Rosh Hashana he held his most spectacular concert ever, in the presence of Queen Isabella and leading figures of the Inquisition. Despite it being Rosh Hashana, the secret Jews dared not miss it, for fear their absence would be noticed. It was a symphonic extravaganza, featuring every musical instrument from every nation throughout the world. Then came the finalé. Don Fernando Aguilar raised his baton, and the powerful notes of tekia, shevarim and terua sounded throughout the auditorium. The church and royal dignitaries cheered the exotic sounds – and the conversos in the audience held back their tears as they heard the sound of the shofar.

9th SEDRA IN:

דְּבָרִים

Devarim

BY NUMBERS:

30 verses
1,484 words
5,652 letters

HEADLINES:

Command to write a Sefer Torah

Parasha Summary

Moses concludes his farewell speech to the Children of Israel, saying: "I am 120 years old today. God has told me that I shall not pass over into the Promised Land. Still, God will pass before you. God will destroy the nations so that you can take possession of the land." Then Moses calls for Joshua, to bless him as he transfers leadership of the people to him. Finally God commands Moses to prepare for his death, and then God Himself blesses Joshua, saying: "Be steadfast and strong! For you are to bring the children of Israel to the land that I have sworn to them, and I will be with you."

YOM KIPPUR IN ISRAEL

I ask myself what makes *Yom Kippur* here in Israel unique compared to those I have known in other places. The most obvious difference here is that it is not only a religious holiday, but it involves everyone in the country. Although we may not all be religious to the same degree, there is a common sharing and a tradition in being together...

Netta Kaplan

QUOTE OF THE WEEK

On the fast of *Yom Kippur*, we examine our souls, recognise our shortcomings and make resolutions for the future. Whilst our introspection is intensely personal, the language of our prayers is intentionally plural, such as 'We have sinned' and 'Remember us for life'. We reach beyond ourselves, acutely aware of the needs of society and the environment of which we are a part.

Chief Rabbi Mirvis

For extra on these articles & more visit www.theus.org.uk/shabbatshalom

YOM KIPPUR IN THE TEMPLE

In ancient times the day was celebrated in the form of a massive public ceremony set in the Temple in Jerusalem. The holiest man in Israel, the High Priest, entered the most sacred space, the Holy of Holies, confessed the sins of the nation using the holiest name of God, and secured atonement for all Israel. It was a moment of intense drama in the life of a people who believed, however fitfully, that their fate depended on their relationship with God, who knew that there is no life, let alone a nation, without sin, and who knew from their history that sin could be punished by catastrophe.

It was a glittering spectacle, the closest of encounters between man and God at the supreme intersection of sacred time and space. The service itself was long and elaborate. The High Priest would be rehearsed in his rituals for seven days beforehand. Five times on the day itself he would have to immerse himself in a *mikva* (ritual bath) and change his robes: gold for his public appearances, plain white for his ministrations within the Holy of Holies. Three times he would make confession, first for himself and his family, then for his fellow priests, and finally for the people as a whole. Each time he used the holy name of God, the watching crowd would prostrate themselves, falling on their faces.

Rabbi Jonathan Sacks, *Ceremony & Celebration*

YOM KIPPUR QUIZ

1. What is the meal before *Yom Kippur* called?
2. Including not eating and drinking, how many prohibitions are there on *Yom Kippur*?
3. What special garment do some men wear on *Yom Kippur*?
4. What is the unique first service of *Yom Kippur*?
5. What do people do when reciting *Viddui*, the lists of sins?
6. What is the *Avoda* service on *Yom Kippur*?
7. During Temple times, two goats were selected on *Yom Kippur*. One was sacrificed for Israel's sins. Where was the other sent?
8. The story of which prophet is read as the *haftara* during *Mincha* on *Yom Kippur*?
9. The last service of *Yom Kippur* is called *Neila* (closing or locking). What is closing at this time?
10. What do we traditionally do immediately after *Yom Kippur* having broken our fast?

Answers:
1. *Seuda Mafseket*
2. Five
3. *Kittel*
4. *Kol Nidrei*
5. Stand and symbolically beat their chests after mentioning each sin
6. The sacrifice ritual in the Temple
7. To the desert
8. Jonah
9. The gates to Heaven, and with it our last chance of the day for our prayers to reach God
10. Start to build the sukka

10th SEDRA IN:

דְּבָרִים

Devarim

BY NUMBERS:

52 verses
614 words
2,326 letters

HEADLINES:

The 'song of history'

Parasha Summary

Most of *Ha'azinu* is a song which talks of the future of the Jewish people and their unbreakable connection to God in particular. Moses affirms that Joshua will succeed him and implores the people to continue observing the *Torah*, as they prepare to cross into the Land of Israel. God tells Moses to ascend Mount Nebo and view the Land before he passes away.

PARASHA QUIZ

1. What symbol is most commonly used in Ha'azinu to describe God? How many times does it appear?

2. God was going to destroy the Israelites because of their sins but then decided not to. Why?

3. Who stood next to Moses when he sang this song?

4. After Moses finished his song, what did he command the people to do?

5. Where did God tell Moses to go in order to die?

6. Why was Moses not allowed to enter the land?

Answers:

1. God is described as a rock six times in Moses' song (32:4, 15, 18, 30, 31, 37)

2. Because the nations of the world would think that they were strong and Israel's God was weak, and would not understand this was merely a punishment for the Israelites (32:27)

3. Joshua bin Nun (32:44)

4. To listen to all he had said that day and to teach their children to observe God's laws (32:46)

5. Mount Nebo in Moab, within view of Jericho (32:49)

6. Because he failed to sanctify God's name when the people asked for water, and struck the rock instead of talking to it as he was commanded to do (32:51)

For extra on these articles & more visit www.theus.org.uk/shabbatshalom

PERSONALITY OF THE WEEK
VILNA GAON

Rabbi Eliyahu ben Shlomo Zalman (1720–1792), more commonly known as the Vilna Gaon (or the Gra, an abbreviation), was the foremost leader of the Jewish community in Europe. Growing up in Vilna, Lithuania, he was identified as a child genius. He was giving public lectures at the age of 7 and outgrew his teachers when he was 10, continuing his education independently from then on.

His diligence and commitment to learning was unsurpassable. His son testified that for 50 years his father did not sleep for more than two hours in a 24-hour period. His breadth of knowledge was astounding – for example, he could state from memory the number of times any sage was mentioned in any particular tractate of the *Talmud*. He was a world-renowned scholar in both *Talmud* and *kabbala*, and also considered secular knowledge to be a vital pursuit of great importance. He was knowledgeable in many secular fields and authored books on grammar and mathematics.

The Vilna Gaon dreamed of living in Israel. He actually began the journey at one point but was unable to complete the trip. Ten years after he passed away, many of his leading students followed in their master's footsteps and settled in the Land of Israel, at a time when the journey was treacherous and life there was exceedingly hard.

The Vilna Gaon passed away in 1797. He left a tremendous legacy, both from his writings on an array of *Torah* subjects and from his outstanding students, who went on to spread *Torah* throughout the people of Israel.

A STORY FOR SHABBAT

The righteousness and kindness of the Vilna Gaon were legendary. Despite his personal poverty, he always gave 20% of his income to charity. He would give his personal money to a pressing need in the community, such as marrying off an orphaned girl or redeeming a captive.

The city of Vilna paid a small monthly stipend to the Gaon, but it became clear to him that the man who was responsible for delivering this money was taking some for himself due to his own poverty-stricken circumstances. The Gaon never let on that he knew and never accused the person of the misdeed, because he did not want to shame him. We would never even have known of this incident, had the guilty man not confessed on his deathbed.

SEDRA:

וְזֹאת הַבְּרָכָה

Vezot Haberacha

11th SEDRA IN:

דְּבָרִים

Devarim

BY NUMBERS:

41 verses
512 words
1,969 letters

HEADLINES:

Moses' final blessing. He is succeeded by Joshua

PERSONALITY OF THE WEEK
SIR MARTIN GILBERT CBE (1936–2015)

Internationally known, Sir Martin Gilbert was a British historian of the 20th century who infused his histories with the voices of those who had lived it – and wove in the Jewish story, making it an integral part of world history. Sir Martin was a pioneer in creating graphic historical atlases, in which each map told a story, and a pioneer in including eyewitness accounts of Holocaust survivors in his work, while encouraging survivors to publish their own memoirs.

Sir Martin's multi-volume biography of Winston Churchill holds the Guinness record for the longest biography and is the basis for any authentic scholarly work on Churchill. Sir Martin also wrote comprehensive histories of both world wars, 12 books on the Shoah and 14 on Israeli and Jewish history. His books have been translated into 24 languages.

Visiting Jews in the former Soviet Union in the 1980s, Sir Martin became a tireless worker for their right to move to Israel. He kept their photos on his bookshelves so he could not forget them. When families were finally allowed to leave, he would spend Friday mornings driving around Jerusalem delivering fresh *challa* to them.

Lady Gilbert

QUOTE OF THE WEEK

The Jewish story, despite its moments of sadness, internal divisions, war and suffering – sometimes terrible suffering – reveals the tenacity of the Jewish people's survival and achievement, its communal life and creativity, and the attempt by each generation to follow the advice which Moses transmitted from God to the Children of Israel, as recorded in the Book of Deuteronomy: 'I have set before you life and death, blessing and cursing: therefore choose life, that both you and your descendants may live.' The injunction 'choose life' became the Jewish religious, communal and national imperative.

Sir Martin Gilbert

DISCUSSION QUESTIONS

1. Why is the experience of Soviet Jewry important for us today?

2. How do you think you can find faith in God through Jewish history?

3. How do you think Jews 'choose life'?

For extra on these articles & more visit www.theus.org.uk/shabbatshalom

Parasha Summary

Vezot Haberacha is the only *parasha* not read in the regular *Shabbat* cycle. Instead it is read on *Simchat Torah* when we conclude and immediately restart the annual *Torah* reading cycle. It recounts the blessings that Moses gave to each of the twelve tribes of Israel and general blessings to the people as a whole. At God's instruction Moses climbs Mount Nevo on the eastern bank of the River Jordan and miraculously shows Moses the Land. God confirms that the Jewish people will inherit the Land. Moses passes away; his burial place remains unknown. No prophet as great as Moses will arise. The second part of the *Tanach* (Hebrew Bible) will open with the Book of Joshua.

JEWISH HISTORY
SIMCHAT TORAH IN 1663

On 14 October 1663 Samuel Pepys, the famous diarist, visited the Spanish and Portuguese Synagogue in Creechurch Lane in the City of London.

Pepys had previously attended a simple synagogue in a private house belonging to a successful Portuguese Jewish merchant, Antonio Fernandez Carvajal, in 1659. It was for Carvajal's memorial service and that occasion had been sombre and decorous.

His second synagogue visit, however, left him scandalised. He wrote in his diary:

"... After dinner my wife and I, by Mr. Rawlinson's conduct, to the Jewish Synagogue: where the men and boys in their vayles [*tallitot*], and the women behind a lattice out of sight; and some things stand up, which I believe is their Law, in a press [the Ark] to which all coming in do bow; and at the putting on their vayles do say something, to which others that hear him do cry Amen, and the party do kiss his vayle. Their service all in a singing way, and in Hebrew. And anon their Laws that they take out of the press are carried by several men, four or five several burthens in all, and they do relieve one another; and whether it is that everyone desires to have the carrying of it, I cannot tell, thus they carried it round about the room while such a service is singing ... But, Lord! To see the disorder, laughing, sporting, and no attention, but confusion in all their service, more like brutes than people knowing the true God, would make a man forswear ever seeing them more and indeed I never did see so much, or could have imagined there had been any religion in the whole world so absurdly performed as this."

Poor Pepys. No one told him that the day he visited was probably *Simchat Torah*! He had never seen in a house of worship anything like the exuberant joy of the day when we dance with the *Sefer Torah* as if the world was a wedding and the *Sefer Torah* a bride, with the same joy as King David when he brought the Holy Ark into Jerusalem.

Sedra calendar

Bereishit		26th October 2019	17th October 2020	2nd October 2021	22nd October 2022
Noach		2nd November 2019	24th October 2020	9th October 2021	29th October 2022
Lech Lecha		9th November 2019	31st October 2020	16th October 2021	5th November 2022
Vayera		16th November 2019	7th November 2020	23rd October 2021	12th November 2022
Chayei Sarah		23rd November 2019	14th November 2020	30th October 2021	19th November 2022
Toledot		30th November 2019	21st November 2020	6th November 2021	26th November 2022
Vayeitzei		7th December 2019	28th November 2020	13th November 2021	3rd December 2022
Vayishlach		14th December 2019	5th December 2020	20th November 2021	10th December 2022
Vayeishev		21st December 2019	12th December 2020	27th November 2021	17th December 2022
Mikeitz		28th December 2019	19th December 2020	4th December 2021	24th December 2022
Vayigash		4th January 2020	26th December 2020	11th December 2021	31st December 2022
Vayechi		11th January 2020	2nd January 2021	18th December 2021	7th January 2023
Shemot		18th January 2020	9th January 2021	25th December 2021	14th January 2023
Vaera		25th January 2020	16th January 2021	1st January 2022	21st January 2023
Bo		1st February 2020	23rd January 2021	8th January 2022	28th January 2023
Beshalach		8th February 2020	30th January 2021	15th January 2022	4th February 2023
Yitro		15th February 2020	6th February 2021	22nd January 2022	11th February 2023
Mishpatim		22nd February 2020	13th February 2021	29th January 2022	18th February 2023
Terumah		29th February 2020	20th February 2021	5th February 2022	25th February 2023
Tetzaveh		7th March 2020	27th February 2021	12th February 2022	4th March 2023
Ki Tisa		14th March 2020	6th March 2021	19th February 2022	11th March 2023
Vayakhel	2nd March 2019	21st March 2020*	13th March 2021*	26th February 2022	18th March 2023*
Pekudei	9th March 2019	21st March 2020*	13th March 2021*	5th March 2022	18th March 2023*
Vayikra	16th March 2019	28th March 2020	20th March 2021	12th March 2022	25th March 2023
Tzav	23rd March 2019	4th April 2020	27th March 2021	19th March 2022	1st April 2023
Shemini	30th March 2019	18th April 2020	10th April 2021	26th March 2022	15th April 2023
Tazria	6th April 2019	25th April 2020*	17th April 2021*	2nd April 2022	22nd April 2023*

* Denotes a double sedra

Sedra calendar

Metzora	13th April 2019	25th April 2020*	17th April 2021*	9th April 2022	22nd April 2023*
Acharei Mot	4th May 2019	2nd May 2020*	24th April 2021*	30th April 2022	29th April 2023*
Kedoshim	11th May 2019	2nd May 2020*	24th April 2021*	7th May 2022	29th April 2023*
Emor	18th May 2019	9th May 2020	1st May 2021	14th May 2022	6th May 2023
Behar	25th May 2019	16th May 2020*	8th May 2021*	21st May 2022	13th May 2023*
Bechukotai	1st June 2019	16th May 2020*	8th May 2021*	28th May 2022	13th May 2023*
Bemidbar	8th June 2019	23rd May 2020	15th May 2021	4th June 2022	20th May 2023
Nasso	15th June 2019	6th June 2020	22nd May 2021	11th June 2022	3rd June 2023
Beha'alotecha	22nd June 2019	13th June 2020	29th May 2021	18th June 2022	10th June 2023
Shelach Lecha	29th June 2019	20th June 2020	5th June 2021	25th June 2022	17th June 2023
Korach	6th July 2019	27th June 2020	12th June 2021	2nd July 2022	24th June 2023
Chukat	13th July 2019	4th July 2020*	19th June 2021	9th July 2022	1st July 2023*
Balak	20th July 2019	4th July 2020*	26th June 2021	16th July 2022	1st July 2023*
Pinchas	27th July 2019	11th July 2020	3rd July 2021	23rd July 2022	8th July 2023
Matot	3rd August 2019*	18th July 2020*	10th July 2021*	30th July 2022*	15th July 2023*
Masei	3rd August 2019*	18th July 2020*	10th July 2021*	30th July 2022*	15th July 2023*
Devarim	10th August 2019	25th July 2020	17th July 2021	6th August 2022	22nd July 2023
Vaetchanan	17th August 2019	1st August 2020	24th July 2021	13th August 2022	29th July 2023
Eikev	24th August 2019	8th August 2020	31st July 2021	20th August 2022	5th August 2023
Re'eh	31st August 2019	15th August 2020	7th August 2021	27th August 2022	12th August 2023
Shofetim	7th September 2019	22nd August 2020	14th August 2021	3rd September 2022	19th August 2023
Ki Teitzei	14th September 2019	29th August 2020	21st August 2021	10th September 2022	26th August 2023
Ki Tavo	21st September 2019	5th September 2020	28th August 2021	17th September 2022	2nd September 2023
Nitzavim	28th September 2019	12th September 2020*	4th September 2021	24th September 2022	9th September 2023*
Vayeilech	5th October 2019	12th September 2020*	11th September 2021	1st October 2022	9th September 2023*
Ha'azinu	12th October 2019	26th September 2020	18th September 2021	8th October 2022	23rd September 2023
Vezot Haberacha	22nd October 2019	11th October 2020	29th September 2021	18th October 2022	8th October 2023

Please note: All dates above (other than Vezot Haberacha) are Saturdays

Picture credits

Credits

Page 12: Operation Solomon - Israel National Photo Collection (INPC), Tsvika Israeli D205-114; page 17: Koren Publishers Jerusalem; page 37: Natan & Avital Sharansky, Shimon Peres, Yitzchak Shamir – INPC, Nati Harnik, D346-037; page 46: Esther Cailingold – courtesy of the Cailingold family; page 51 – Øyvind Holmstad (Wikimedia Commons); page 57 – courtesy of Sivan Rahav Meir; page 72: IDF paratroopers at the Western Wall – INPC, D327-042; page 91: courtesy of University Jewish Chaplaincy; page 102: The Chief Rabbi's Ma'ayan Programme - courtesy of the Office of the Chief Rabbi (OCR); page 105: courtesy of the OCR; p.108: Rabbi Soloveitchik – courtesy of Yeshiva University, New York ; page 113: courtesy of the Office of Rabbi Sacks; page 118: courtesy of Lady Gilbert.

Shutterstock Credits

P4...........Parasha - Triff/Shutterstock.com
P5............Shabbat - Rawpixel.com/Shutterstock.com
P6...........Parasha - Nikki Zalewski/Shutterstock.com
P6...........The Flood Story - Sanit Fuangnakhon/Shutterstock.com
P9...........Kindertransport - Uwe Aranas/Shutterstock.com
P9...........Parasha - Alefbet/Shutterstock.com
P10........Parasha - Bgsmith/Shutterstock.com
P11..........Rambam - Vkilikov/Shutterstock.com
P11..........Story - Aleksei Verhovski/Shutterstock.com
P12........Beta Israel - Kobby Dagan/Shutterstock.com
P14........Mount Moriah - David Ionut/Shutterstock.com
P15........Power Of Youth (Both Pictures) - Photo 1 Fotokon, Photo 2 Northfoto/Shutterstock.com
P16........Parasha - Costas Anton Dumitrescu/Shutterstock.com
P17........Discussion Questions - Oksana Mizina/Shutterstock.com
P18........Questions - Digitalfabiani/Shutterstock.com
P19........The First Kibbutz - Everett Historical/Shutterstock.com
P20........Parasha - Zapomicron/Shutterstock.com
P24........Parasha - Saiko3p/Shutterstock.com
P27........Parasha Quiz - Roman Yanushevsky/Shutterstock.com
P32........Parasha - Artlight Production/Shutterstock.com
P33........Parasha Quiz - Khazanova/Shutterstock.com
P36........Parasha - Masha Arkulis/Shutterstock.com
P36........Dvar Torah (Girl With Seedlings) - Yuganov Konstantin/Shutterstock.com
P38........Parasha - Masha Arkulis/Shutterstock.com
P40........Personality Of The Week - Marzolino/Shutterstock.com
P41........Technion University - The World In Hdr/Shutterstock.com
P43........A Story For Shabbat - Aless/Shutterstock.com
P44........Dvar Torah - Airdone/Shutterstock.com
P45........Shabbat Kiddush - Rhonda Roth/Shutterstock.com
P50........Dvar Torah - Tomertu/Shutterstock.com
P54........Parasha - Frolova_elena/Shutterstock.com
P55........Esther - Tomertu/Shutterstock.com
P56........Parasha - Studio Evasion/Shutterstock.com

P59........Israel Geography - Elena Dijour/Shutterstock.com
P60........Parasha - Alena Sli/Shutterstock.com
P62........Parasha - Styleuneed.de/Shutterstock.com
P62........Israel Geography - Evanessa/Shutterstock.com
P63........Shabbat Quiz - Lisa Kolbasa/Shutterstock.com
P63........Jewish History - Irisphoto1/Shutterstock.com
P66........Parasha - Chinnapong/Shutterstock.com
P67........A Story For Shabbat - Rawpixel.com/Shutterstock.com
P68........Israel - Chameleonseye/Shutterstock.com
P70........Parasha - Protasov An/Shutterstock.com
P70........A Story For Shabbat - Fcg/Shutterstock.com
P71........Israel - Pattanachai W/Shutterstock.com
P72........Parasha - Elena Shashkina/Shutterstock.com
P73........Dvar Torah - Lana Samcorp/Shutterstock.com
P76........Shavuot In Israel - Vladislav Noseek/Shutterstock.com
P77........Giving Of The Torah - James Steidl/Shutterstock.com
P79........Quiz - Tomertu/Shutterstock.com
P81........Quote Of The Week - Lev Radin/Shutterstock.com
P82........Dvar Torah - Jekli/Shutterstock.com
P83........A Shabbat Story - Tomertu/Shutterstock.com
P83........Parasha Quiz - Studio Evasion/Shutterstock.com
P86........Dvar Torah - Scottchan/Shutterstock.com
P94........Shabbat Story - Rudmer Zwerver/Shutterstock.com
P101......Quiz - Kavram/Shutterstock.com
P104......Parasha– Tomertu/Shutterstock.com
P105......Jewish History - Everett Historical/Shutterstock.com
P106......Dvar Torah - Barabasa/Shutterstock.com
P107......A Story For Shabbat - Galyna_p/Shutterstock.com
P112......Parasha - Wavebreakmedia/Shutterstock.com
P112......The Jewish Calendar In Israel - Maja H./Shutterstock.com
P114......Parasha - Guy Zidel/Shutterstock.com
P115......Yom Kippur Quiz - Arturo Escorza Pedraza/Shutterstock.com
P116......Parasha - Rndms/Shutterstock.com